Shirley Temple Dolls
and COLLECTIBLES

Shirley Temple Dolls
and COLLECTIBLES

by
Patricia R. Smith

All photographs by Dwight F. Smith, unless noted

EDITOR: Karen Penner

COLLECTOR BOOKS

Published by Collector Books
Box 3009
Paducah, Kentucky, 42001

Distributed by

Crown Publishers, Inc.

1 Park Ave.
New York, New York 10016

DEDICATION

This book is dedicated to all who lived through the 1930's, and to all those who felt like they did because they heard so much about it! Shirley Temple brought pleasure to an unhappy world; she was born at the "right time" to affect millions of lives with her sweet smile and helped make them forget their own tears.

The author wishes to thank some very special people as this book could not have been compiled without them. The first is Mr. and Mrs. Earl (Marge) Meisinger. Marge is dedicated to collecting Shirley Temple memorabilia because of her love of the subject. She is a researcher of her subject and unique, in that she wants to share her collecting and knowledge with others. Marge's husband, Earl, helps and we all hope that he never looses his "beginners" luck. The second special person is Mary Stuecher, whose entire being is *love*

that overflowed on a little girl of the 1930's, Shirley Temple. Mary is a lady who also is helped by her husband, who with much love and a sense of humor even admires her talent "to play with dolls." Mary has a great talent to recreate the Shirley wardrobes to help collectors who are unable to locate the originals. Both these ladies collections are much too extensive for just one book and we had to pick and choose examples from them. Hopefully, at a later date, we shall be able to continue with a Volume II.

We would also like to thank Dorothy Cassidy, John Axe, Shirley Bertrand, Kay Bransky, Sandy Crump, Roberta Lago, Mandeville-Barkel Collection, Violet Meynen, and Pauline Minnick for the use of their Shirley Temple and related items.

ALL ITEMS FROM
THE MEISINGER COLLECTION UNLESS NOTED.

OTHER BOOKS BY AUTHOR
Modern Collector's Dolls: Vol. I, II & III
Antique Collector's Dolls: Vol. I & II
Armand Marseille's Dolls
Kestner & Simon & Halbig Dolls
Collector's Teen Dolls

Earl and Marge Meisinger, shown with their favorite Shirley Temple Doll, "The Little Colonel"

Mary Stuecher known as Mistress Mary to the Shirley Temple collectors.

CONTENTS

Because the content pages are so complete, there will be no index included in this book.

THE SHIRLEY TEMPLE STORY

by Mary Stuecher

"If I had one wish to make,
This is the wish I would choose:
I'd want an old straw hat,
A suit of overalls,
And a worn-out pair of shoes."1

36" Vinyl Shirley Temple marked Ideal Doll/ST-35-2, on the head and Ideal (in oval)/35-5, on back. Redressed as "Rebecca of Sunnybrook Farm." (Courtesy Mary Stuecher)

These are the words Shirley Temple sang as she danced with Bill Robinson in the movie, *Rebecca of Sunnybrook Farm*. To thousands of viewers, wearing *their* shabby clothes and worn-out shoes, seated in darkened theaters across the country, Shirley herself was the stuff wishes were made of—a delightful relief from the reality of the dark and dreary depression days.

She was "Curly Top," "Bright Eyes," "The Little Princess"—her twinkling toes and dimpled smile melted the hearts of the very young, and the very old, and everyone in between.

When Shirley Jane Temple was born on April 23, 1928, in Santa Monica, California, little did her parents dream that they had begotten a child who would influence the next decade more than any other child in this century.

George and Gertrude Temple were delighted to have a daughter to join their family of two sons, Jack, twelve years old, and George, Jr., called Sonny, who was eight. Shirley turned out to be a real charmer, appealingly chubby and dimpled, with golden curls to match her loving, sunny disposition.

When Mrs. Temple enrolled three year old Shirley in a dancing class, fate stepped in. A talent scout for Educational Pictures visited the dance studio in his search for children to be featured in one reel spoofs of adult films called *Baby Burlesks*, and from among the parade of youngsters, Shirley was picked. After the diaper-clad roles for *Baby Burlesks* were completed, Shirley made a series of short films called *Frolics of Youth*. While attending the preview of the fourth picture of this series, Jay Gorney, of Fox Film Corporation, asked Mrs. Temple to bring Shirley over to test for *Stand Up and Cheer*, a movie ready to go into production. The movie called for a little girl to sing and dance with Jimmy Dunn.

Shirley tested for the part and the rest is history. When people across the nation saw the movie, they didn't ask their friends, "Have you seen *Stand Up and Cheer?* but rather, "Have you seen the little Shirley Temple?" The song and dance routine that brought Shirley fame was "Baby, Take a Bow."

The next step on her stairway to stardom was her loan out to Paramount Studios for the Damon Runyon story, *Little Miss Marker*. Her role of "Marky" established Shirley as a delightful little actress and proved there was more to this appealing child than cuteness and an ability to respond to rhythm.

Fox recognized the potential their little starlet held and signed her to a long term contract. She was soon given starring roles in the pictures that followed—some remakes of old successful films; others, written and adapted just for Shirley and her talents.

Across the nation movie goers eagerly awaited each new Temple film, causing Shirley to rise to first place at the Box Office by 1936, and remain there for three years. Shirley's popularity knew no bounds. She was showered with gifts, honors, and attention from her admirers throughout the world. Her hairdo, dress, and mannerisms were widely copied. Curious why crowds gathered to stare at her, she was told they liked her because she was polite and friendly, had a clean face and hands, and looked happy.

Shirley items of an unbelievable assortment appeared to the delight of her public.

She was the most photographed celebrity of the era, and pictures of her appeared daily in publications somewhere around the world. Any news about her, whether she sustained a small "black eye" in a studio fall or her pet dog ran away, was of international interest.

Other studios sought Shirley's services, but Twentieth Century Fox held on to their prize. Metro Goldwyn Mayer negotiated to use Shirley in a movie they were planning in exchange for Jean Harlow. When Jean died suddenly and tragically, the deal was called off, and a little girl named Frances Gumm was given her chance at stardom. We know her better as Judy Garland, and the movie, *The Wizard of Oz*.

Oddly enough the bubble burst and the fairytale ended in 1940, when Shirley did star in a fairytale, *The Bluebird*. This extravagant fantasy did not appeal to Shirley's fans. If one takes time to analyze it, this was not a picture that did justice to Shirley's kind of talent, and the expected light heartedness and warm appeal were lacking in this film.

Her next film, *Young People*, prophetically dealt with the retirement of a vaudeville family and its acceptance as "Just plain folks."

Shirley's affiliation with Twentieth Century Fox was ended by mutual consent of her parents and the studio. It was at this time that Shirley, on what she thought was her twelfth birthday, was "given back" the year the studio had lopped off her age when she first was put under contract.

Up to this time her education had been supplied by the studio and its special teachers. Now she was enrolled at

Westlake School for Girls where she was given the chance for a normal education and the close friendships most teenage girls enjoy. Shirley was soon accepted as "one of the gang," not because of *who* she was, but because of *what* she was.

Deserved credit must be given to her parents and the studio for carefully nurturing Shirley's personality, and for not turning out a pampered, self-centered "movie brat."

She was not the "goody-two-shoes" many articles during her reign as America's Princess would have readers believe. On most occasions she exhibited very normal behavior. One of the favorite stories she tells on herself involved the wife of the President of the United States. During a trip east, Shirley and her parents were invited to the Roosevelt Hyde Park home for a barbeque. Mrs. Roosevelt herself presided over the hamburgers. Shirley, carrying a little white lace purse, had hidden inside one of her favorite "toys"—a sling shot. Unable to resist temptation as Mrs. Roosevelt bent over tending the hamburgers, she picked up a little pebble, aimed, and hit on target. The flurry of excitement this caused gave Shirley ample time to replace the offending object in her purse. Unfortunately, this deed was noticed by her mother, who applied proper discipline when they returned to their hotel.

Shirley's retirement was heralded by features in newspapers and magazines throughout the world, but it was short lived, for she was back in front of the cameras in little more than a year. MGM negotiated a contract, and starred her in *Kathleen*, a typical "Shirleyesque" film. This was followed by a teenage vehicle for United Artists, *Miss Annie Rooney*, in which she received her first romantic screen kiss.

When she was put under contract to David O. Selznik in 1943, and reintroduced to the public as teenage Brig in the war-time drama, *Since You Went Away*, great things in her career were expected. Selznik didn't really do much with the blossoming Shirley, and as a result she studio-hopped, making a variety of movies, mostly light-hearted and in the comedy vein.

Regardless, Shirley's fans did not desert her; their interest in her growing up, dating, and finding young love did not wane. Their devotion to her is clearly evident as one views the mountains of publicity, pictures, advertisements, and fan letters that flowed during the forties.

In 1945 young love blossomed into engagement and marriage at seventeen to John Agar, a sergeant in the Army Air Forces. With the birth of Linda Susan in January, 1948, shortly before Shirley's own twentieth birthday, the public, teary-eyed and sentimental, finally had to accept the fact that "their baby" had truly grown up.

The dream turned into nightmare, and the young Shirley, who had so optimistically proclaimed, "No Hollywood divorce for this child," had to eat her words.

Crushed by the events in her life, Shirley found renewal in Hawaii, one of her favorite places since childhood, and there met the man with whom she would find lasting happiness, Charles Alden Black. With this marriage, Shirley retired from the movie world, and led the fulfilling life of homemaker and mother to Susan and the children of this marriage, Charles Jr. and Lori. Only occasional glimpses of her private life had to suffice for her fans until 1957.

Movies found a new outlet in the popular new medium of television. With reruns of Shirley's movies gaining new audiences, she did a TV series of her own, *Shirley Temple Story-Book*, and shortly after a second series, *The Shirley Temple Show*. Both were so successful that the Shirley dolls, books, games, dresses, and other assorted items that had been so popular during her childhood were reissued.

As an adult Shirley has frequently been spotlighted in the public eye. In her community she took an active part in charity and service projects. She traveled extensively on behalf of the Multiple Schlerosis Foundation.

In 1967 she ran unsuccessfully as candidate for the Republican nomination to Congress for California's Eleventh District. Enjoying this "second career" in public service, she was appointed delegate to the United Nations General Assembly in 1969 and served diligently. From 1972 to 1974 she worked as special assistant to the chairman of the President's Council for Environmental Quality. In the fall of 1974 she was named United States Ambassador to Ghana, Africa.

But it was in her personal life that Shirley performed a beautiful and unselfish act. Supported by a loving family and confident in God's daily care, Shirley underwent breast cancer surgery in November, 1972. She courageously announced this news to the press in the hope that other women would be encouraged to face the problem and "not stay home and be afraid." The response was tremendous. Thousands poured out their love, admiration, and thanks to the adult Shirley in letters, cards, and telegrams.

Gertrude Temple, Shirley's ambitious and devoted mother, instilled early in Shirley a sense of obligation to her public, a desire to please and serve others. Shirley's only selfishness is for her family privacy, and for this she cannot be criticized. In one of the early articles on bringing up Shirley, Mrs. Temple wrote that her deepest wish was that Shirley would grow into a lovable woman of character, faith and usefulness. Who of us would dare deny that Mrs. Temple's wish came true!

The latest happening in the life of Shirley Temple Black is that she was named new Protocol Chief to the White House. Mrs. Black, appointed by President Ford, is the first woman to hold the position in charge of pomp and pageantry for visiting foreign leaders and diplomats to the White House.

Shirley Temple Black at 48, is the mother of three, has been ambassador to Ghana since September 1974. She earlier was a special presidential assistant to Richard M. Nixon on environmental matters and served as the U.S. delegate to the United Nations General Assembly.

1"An Old Straw Hat," words and music by Mack Gordon and Harry Revel, published by Leo Feist, Inc., 1629 Broadway, N.Y., N.Y. (1938) Used by permission.

SHIRLEY TEMPLE MOVIES
BY THE YEAR

1932: The Runt Page. Educational Films, Inc. (10 min. film)
War Babies. Educational Films Corp. (A "short" film)
The Pie-Covered Wagon. Educational Films Corp.
Glad Rags To Riches. Educational Films Corp. (Sang first song)
The Kid's Last Stand. Educational Films Corp.
Polly-Tix In Washington. Educational Films Corp.
Kiddin' Hollywood. Educational Films Corp.
Kiddin' Africa. Educational Films Corp.
1933: The Red-Haired Alibi. Tower Productions, Inc.
Merrily Yours. Educational Films Corp.
Out All Night. Universal
Dora's Dunking Doughnuts. Educational Films Corp.
Pardon My Pups. Educational Films Corp.
Managed Money. Educational Films Corp.
What To Do? Educational Films Corp.
To The Last Man. Paramount
1934: Carolina. Fox Film Corp.
New Deal Rhythm. Paramount
Change Of Heart. Fox Film Corp.
Mandalay. First National
Little Miss Marker. Paramount
Bottoms Up. Fox Film Corp.
Stand Up And Cheer. Fox Film Corp.
Now I'll Tell. Fox Film Corp.
Baby Take a Bow. Fox Film Corp.
Now And Forever. Paramount
Bright Eyes. Fox Film Corp.
The Little Colonel. Fox Films Corp.
1935: Our Little Girl. Fox Films Corp.

Curly Top. Fox Films Corp.
The Littlest Rebel. Twentieth Century Fox
1936: Captain January. Twentieth Century-Fox
The Poor Little Rich Girl. Twentieth Century-Fox
Dimples. Twenieth Century-Fox
Stowaway. Twenieth Century-Fox
1937: Wee Willie Winkie. Twentieth Century-Fox
Heidi. Twentieth Century-Fox
1938: Rebecca Of Sunnybrook Farm. Twentieth Century Fox
Just Around the Corner. Twentieth Century-Fox
Little Miss Broadway. Twentieth Century-Fox
1939: The Little Princess. Twentieth Century-Fox
Susannah Of The Mounties. Twentieth Century-Fox
1940: The Blue Bird. Twentieth Century-Fox
Young People. Twentieth Century-Fox
1941: Kathleen. Metro-Goldwyn-Mayer
1942: Miss Annie Rooney. United Artists
1943: Since You Went Away. United Artists
I'll Be Seeing You. United Artists
1945: Kiss And Tell. Columbia
1946: Honeymoon. RKO
The Bachelor and the Bobby Soxer. RKO
1947: That Hagen Girl. Warner Bros.-First National
1948: Fort Apache. Argosy Pictures. RKO release
Adventure In Baltimore. RKO
1949: Mr. Belvedere Goes To College. Twentieth Century-Fox
The Story of Seabiscuit. Warner Bros.

DOLLS

by Mary Stuecher

Shirley Temple's popularity increases yearly. Shirley collectors draw not only from her childhood fans, but from many new and younger collectors. Just witness the vast number of Shirley seekers. Most collectors are as interested in Shirley Temple Black, the woman of today, as they are in Shirley Temple, the child of yesterday. They search diligently to add items to their collections, and seek the latest news about her eagerly.

The number of Shirley items to be sought out is vast indeed. High on the list is the Shirley doll. The first Shirley doll was issued by the Ideal Novelty and Toy Company (later Ideal Toy Corporation). This was in the fall of 1934, and the doll was rushed to the stores in time for Christmas sales. But the doll "discovery" and design must be credited to Mollye Goldman, the founder and sole designer of Mollye Dolls, Hollywood Cinema Fashions and M.G.M. Sales.

Mollye Goldman saw the 1933 film "Merrily Yours" and immediately went home to design clothes for Shirley Temple. She wired a friend, Mr. Morris Michtom, in New York to offer him the Shirley Temple idea. He wired back and sent her a ticket to come to New York and talk about it. His first question, on arrival was "WHAT is a Shirley Temple?"... from this lead to the agreement that Ideal make the dolls (designed by Bernard Lipfert) and Mollye would design and make the doll's clothes. The very first Shirley Temple dresses have a Mollye label.

Mollye Goldman attended all the previews of Shirley Temple movies then designed the clothes for the dolls, with a price range suitable to sell to the stores, for Mollye's style was to be the most elaborate and with quality that would have done a real child great justice. Often the dolls were dressed, sent on to Shirley Temple, then childrens clothes were made from them (Nanette and Cinderella). Mollye Goldman designed and made all the Shirley Temple clothes from 1933 through 1936. Her agreement with Ideal was not honored after 1936.

A word here about the tags on the clothes of that era. (Tags may be found in the black and white section of this book) Many of the early dress tags carry the NRA and a blue eagle. This stood for the National Recovery Administration. This was a former federal agency which was set up under the National Industrial Recovery Act, approved June 16, 1933, and which was dissolved by order of the President on Jan. 1, 1936, after the United States Supreme Court on May 27, 1935 in a unanimous decision, had declared Section 3 of the Title I of the act, its most important provision, unconstitutional.

The NRA was one of the important legislative measures enacted during the early days of the Roosevelt (New Deal) administration for the purpose of combating the economic depression which began in 1929, and in 1933 was at about its worst. This Act was designed to relieve industrial unemployment by shortening hours of labor, increasing wages, and eliminating unfair trade practices as well as destructive price cutting through the enforcement of such codes of fair competition.

President Roosevelt appointed Brig. Gen. Hugh S. Johnson, who had resigned from the Army in 1919, to administer the provisions of Title I of the code (fair competition). While General Johnson was at the helm, NRA was front page news almost daily. He was a picturesque character with a remarkable flair for the dramatic. Throughout the country he made speeches, threatening to "crack down" on those in-dustires who balked at going his way. He adopted the "Blue Eagle" as NRA's emblem; insisted that it be used as a mark of identification on all goods manufactured under code provisions and that all householders display replicas of it in their windows as evidence of their loyalty to the country and as a guarantee that they would purchase only products bearing the insignia. Among the public there was much criticism of the codes.

General Johnson resigned as administrator Sept. 24, 1934 and President Roosevelt created the National Industrial Recovery Board. The actual NRA (and others) were disolved on April 1, 1936. The Shirley Temple doll clothes designed by Mollye Goldman generally have the NRA tag (1933 to 1936) but a few fell on both sides of these dates.

By September of 1935, seven sizes of the little girl Shirley doll was offered, and in addition six sizes of the Shirley baby doll. The girl doll eventually was available in sizes ranging from eleven inches to twenty-seven inches. Over the next six years, over six million Shirley Temple dolls were sold.

Trunk sets in several sizes and a large assortment of extra costumes were offered by Ideal in addition to the dolls.

F.A. Whitney Carriage Company of Leominster, Massachusetts, manufactured a line of Shirley doll buggies.

Many other companies made unauthorized versions of the Shirley Temple doll, finding devious ways to outsmart the copyright laws. These Shirley look-alikes, mostly unmarked, add confusion to the picture, and, as a result, any doll with dimples and a "Shirley" look may be represented as the authentic item.

Ideal used the Shirley molds for other dolls. A case in point is "Marama," the Hurricane doll. The movie, *Hurricane*, was made in 1937 by Sam Goldwyn, Incorporated, starring Jon Hall and Dorothy Lamour. A little doll in the story, was treasured by "Terangie" to remind him of his love for the real "Marama." Although Ideal used the Shirley molds to make this doll, it does *not* represent Shirley Temple in one of her movie roles. Shirley Temple *did not* play in the movie, "Hurricane."

Eventually the Shirley molds were sold to other doll companies, further adding to the confusion.

In 1957 Ideal reissued the Shirley doll with vinyl head, rooted curls, and hard plastic torso and limbs in twelve, fifteen, seventeen, nineteen, and thirty-five inch sizes. A variety of outfits was available for the twelve inch sized doll, most of them a Shirley *type*, rather than authentic movie costumes.

When Montgomery Wards celebrated its 100th Anniversary in 1972, the company again brought out a fifteen inch Shirley doll in vinyl, using the 1957 molds. Wards also put out an early version of the 1937 Shirley, measuring sixteen and one-quarter inches.

The present vinyl issue, on the market since the summer of 1973, measures sixteen and one-half inches and varies slightly from the Wards issue. Although considerable criticism of this doll has been heard, the body modeling is definitely the most realistic of the child Shirley, and the features have an uncanny resemblance to the real life child. Four outfits that are versions of authentic costumes were manufactured for this doll: "Captain January," "Heidi," "Rebecca of Sunnybrook Farm," and the poorest copy, "The Little Colonel."

Every conceivable item bearing Shirley's image or tying up with Shirley's movies and popularity flooded the market in the 1930's.

An entire line of paper dolls, coloring books, scrapbooks, story books, and biographical books was produced by Saalfield Publishing Company of Akron, Ohio.

Cinderella Frocks, bearing the Shirley Temple brand, were manufactured by Rosenau Brothers, Incorporated, of Philadelphia, Pennsylvania. Shirley herself modeled each dress and her picture appeared on the tag identifying the dress. Other articles of wearing apparel, such as anklets, hats, hair ribbons, barrettes, purses, and jewelry were offered.

Picture frames contained her photograph; soap, carnival plaster, and salt glaze figures abounded. Even Shirley Temple candy molds were made.

Western Tablet and Stationery Corporation put out paper tablets and composition books. Pocket mirrors, reels of Shirley film for home use, song books, sheet music, records, cards of curlers, doll dress patterns, sewing sets, and playing cards were available. Shirley herself appeared in many ads for a wide range of items.

The Hazel Atlas Glass Company made cobalt blue glassware for General Mills in 1936 that they offered as free premiums with the purchase of their products, Bisquick and Wheaties. Three items, each bearing a different picture of Shirley, were produced—a pitcher, mug, and bowl. When the order was suddenly cancelled, the remaining glass was used up in two patterns of "depression" glassware, Royal Lace and Moderntone.

Add to all this the wealth of studio photographs, pictures and articles from newspapers and magazines, post cards, theater posters, standees, and lobby displays. And on, and on, and on, and on!

In the fifties, Saalfield revived Shirley Temple paper doll sets. Samuel Gabriel Sons and Company, Incorporated, New York, also put out paper dolls and play sets. Random House published a variety of Shirley related books.

Shirley, along with the editors of *Look* magazine, authored her autobiography, *My Young Life*, in 1945. Over the years she has contributed a number of articles for several magazines.

In 1975, Shirley was honored on Ceres Medals, issued by the Food and Agriculture Organization of the United Nations.

A drawing of her even appears on the cover of 1976 telephone directories!

News items of Shirley memorabilia continue to come to light. For the avid collector the next delightful find may be "Just Around the Corner."

COMPOSITION DOLLS SIZES:

11"	17"	22"
13"	18"	25"
16"	20"	27"

Newspaper ad for Shirley Temple doll 1936

In some catalogues, such as Sears 1934 large Christmas book, a 15½" size is listed, and Butler Bros. of Oct. 1935 offers a 15", and not a 16" is listed. In only one catalog available, could be found a 17" doll in a trunk. There was variation of molds due to the compostion expansion or shrinkage up to 1". 20" dolls have been found with a + mark that actually measure 21" and ones with a — mark that measure 19". One seen has both the plus and minus after the 20 and measures exactly 20". It must also be remembered that the manufacturers measured from the center of the top of the head and most collectors measure from the top of the forehead.

All the dolls are composition and original.
The exception is the largest on the top,
she is the 36" vinyl and plastic Shirley. All
from the collection of Marge Meisinger.

DOLL MARKS

#1. SHIRLEY TEMPLE

#2. SHIRLEY TEMPLE
IDEAL
N. & T. Co.

#3. Shirley Temple

SHIRLEY TEMPLE

#4. Shirley Temple

Vinyl Dolls:
12" — Ideal Doll — head
ST-12-N
ST-12-N — Back

15" — Ideal Doll — head
ST-15-N
ST-15-N — Back

17" — Ideal Doll — head
ST-17-1
Ideal Doll
ST-17- — back

19" — Ideal Doll — head
ST-19-1
Ideal Doll
ST-19 — back

35" — Ideal Doll — head
ST-35-38-2
Ideal
35-5 — back

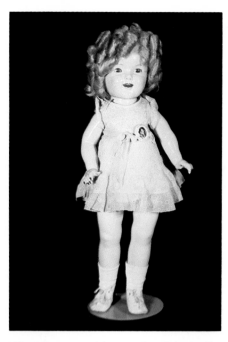

13" All composition and original dimity dress. Marks: #1/13 and head and back. For "Little Miss Marker" 1934 release. Designed by Mollye.

20" All composition and original. For "Dora's Dunking Doughnuts". 1933 release. Rayon tag. Marks: #2 with 20 reversed and backward, on head. #3 and a *, on back. Designed by Mollye.

20" All composition and original. For "Merrily Yours" 1933 release. Cotton dress with woven NRA tag. Marks: #2 with backward 20 over it, on head. #1, on back. 1935. This doll is actually 19" tall. Designed by Mollye.

Shows three versions of original Shirley Temple doll boxes.

11" All composition and original. Dimity dress with rayon tag. From "Stand Up and Cheer." 1934. (End of box only is original) Marks: #1/11, on head and back. This dress also came in red and green. Designed by Mollye.

22" All composition to show the typical Shirley Temple body construction. Marks: #1, on head. #3/22 on back.

Left: 15" All composition and original. Cotton with rayon tag. Flirty eyes. Marks: #1, on head. #1/16, on back although doll measures 15" tall. Right: 13" all composition and all original. Cotton with woven NRA tag. Marks: #2, on head. #1, on back. Both are for "Bright Eyes" 1934. Designed by Mollye.

18" All composition. Organdy blouse and print cotton jumper. Other doll has original velveteen coat and hat with woven NRA tag. Right: marked #2/18, on head. #1/18, on back. Left doll has flirty eyes and is marked: #3/18, on head. #1/18, on back. For "Managed Money" 1933 release. Designed by Mollye.

18" All composition and original. Cotton dresses with woven NRA tag. Marks: Right: #1, on head and back. Left: #1/18, on head. #1, on back. For "Bright Eyes" 1934 release. Designed by Mollye.

27" All composition and original dotted organdy with rayon tag. From "Stand Up and Cheer" 1934. Flirty eyes. No marks on head. #1/27, on back. This dress also came in blue and green. Designed by Mollye.

18" All composition and all original. Rayon tags. Right: Marks: #2/18, on head. #1/18, on back. Left: #3/18, on head. 18, on back. For "Little Miss Marker" 1934 release. Designed by Mollye.

13 3/8" tall trunk of wood that holds 13" doll.

13" All composition and all original in original trunk. Organdy dress from "Curly Top" 1935. Marks: #1/13, on head and back. See following photo of trunk. Clothes designed by Mollye.

20" All composition and original organdy dress from "Curly Top" 1935. Rayon tag. Marks: #2, with backward 20. #3 and a *, on back. Designed by Mollye.

Left: 13" All composition and all original. Cotton dress. Rayon tag. Marks: #1/13, on head. #1, on back. Right: 16" All composition and original. Cotton dress. Rayon tag. Marks: #1/13, on head. #1, on back. Right: 16" All composition and original. Cotton pique dress. Rayon tag. Marks: #2, on head. #1/16, on back. Both are for "Curly Top" 1935. Designed by Mollye.

16" All composition and original. Cotton pique. For "Now and Forever" 1934 release. Rayon tag. Marks: #1/16, on head and back. Also came in white. Designed by Mollye.

18" All composition. Has dark eyeshadow. All original for "Now and Forever" 1934 release. Marks: #1/18, on head. 18/"Ideal" on back. Designed by Mollye. (Courtesy Mary Stuecher)

18" All composition and original. Taffeta dress from "Little Colonel." Dress was available also in yellow, lavender or green taffeta. 1935. Marks: #1/18, on head and back. Designed by Mollye.

16" All composition and all original except bonnet, in original box "Little Colonel" 1935 in organdy with woven NRA tag. Marks: #2, on head. #1/16, on back. Designed by Mollye.

13" All composition and original in original box. "Scotty" dress of pique with rayon tag. For "Our Little Girl" 1935 release. Marks: #1/13, on head and back. Designed by Mollye.

18" All composition and original. Cotton dress from "Our Little Girl" Woven NRA tag. 1935. Marks: #2/18, on head. #1/18, on back. Designed by Mollye.

18" All composition and original. For "Our Little Girl" 1935 release. Dress is cotton. Marks: #3/18, head and back. Designed by Mollye.

25" All composition and all original. Cotton dress for "Our Little Girl" Rayon NRA tag. 1935. Marks: #2, on head. #1/25, on back. Designed by Mollye. (Courtesy Violet Meynen)

11" All composition and original in original box. Organdy dress from "Curly Top" 1935. Rayon tag. Blue tin eyes. Marks: #1/11, on head and back. Designed by Mollye.

13" All composition and original in original box. Organdy "Curly Top" dress. 1935. Rayon tag. Marks: #1/13, on head and back. Also came in aqua. Designed by Mollye.

13" All composition and original organdy dress for "Curly Top." Flirty eyes. Original pin but not for this doll. Marks: #1/13, on head and back. 1935. Designed by Mollye.

18" All composition and original. Cotton dress with rayon NRA tag. For "Curly Top" 1935 release. Marks: #1/18, on head and body. Designed by Mollye.

27" All composition and all original. Organdy dress for "Dimples" 1936 release. Flirty eyes. No mark on head. #1, on back. This doll was used in 1937 ads also. Designed by Mollye.

17" All composition and original. Pink organdy dress as "Baby Take A Bow" 1936. Embroidered collar. Marks: #2, on head. #1/17, on back. See picture of her original trunk on next page. She came in original box inside trunk. Designed by Mollye.

13" All composition and original. Cotton dress. Marks: #1, on head. #1/13, on back. From "Baby Take A Bow" 1936. Designed by Mollye.

18" All composition and original. Cotton dress with woven NRA tag. 1935 "sailboat" dress with applique boat missing. Marks: #1, on head. #1/18, on back. Designed by Mollye for "Curly Top" release 1935.

18" All composition original dress with woven NRA tag. From "Baby Take A Bow" 1936 release. Marks: #2, on head. #3/18, on back. Designed by Mollye.

13" All composition and all original. For "Poor Little Rich Girl" release. Cotton pique dress. Rayon tag. 1936. Marks: #1/13, on head and back. Designed by Mollye.

13" All composition and original in pink organdy. Woven NRA tag. Marks: #2, on head. #3 and a *, on back. For Capt. January" 1936 release. Designed by Mollye.

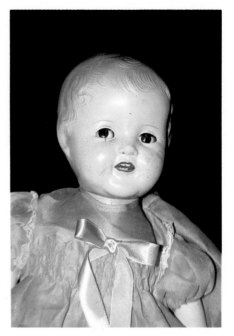

Wood trunk with 17" doll. Also included in trunk are: Blue dotted organdy dress, sunsuit and bonnet. Blue print pajamas. Blue dimity dress with polka dot trim and extra shoes and socks. 1936. This is undoubtedly the most "mint" doll to be found today. Bought from the original owner who never had her out of the box.

16" Shirley Temple baby. Composition swivel head on rubber shoulder plate. Molded hair, flirty brown sleep eyes, open mouth with two upper and three lower teeth. Rubber arms, cloth body and composition legs. Dimples. The baby came with a wig also. Marks: #1, on head. (Courtesy Mary Stuecher)

13" All composition. Brown sleep eyes. In original trunk. Shown in copy of "Baby Take A Bow" outfit. Marks: #1, on head. #1/13, on body. (Courtesy Mary Stuecher)

27" All composition. Original sailor suit with hat and tie missing. From 1936 Captain January. (Courtesy Roberta Lago)

11" Texas Ranger and/or "Cowgirl." Two different versions. Real leather chaps and vests. Cotton plaid shirts. 1936 to coincide with Texas Centennial celebrations. Shirley was named an honorary "Texas Ranger." Left doll has glass eyes and right has tin eyes. Both are marked #1/11, on head and backs. Designed by Mollye.

15

13" All composition and original organdy dress. Woven NRA tag. Marks: #1/13, on head and back. From "Poor Little Rich Girl." 1936.

16" All composition and original as "Heidi" Cotton dress, organdy apron pinafore. Rayon tag. 1937. Marks: #1/60, on head. #1/16, on back.

18" All composition and original (except feather). Marks: #2/18, on head. #3/18, on back. For "Just Around the Corner" 1938 release.

11" All composition. All original from "Susannah Of The Mounties" 1939. Marks: 11/#1, on head and body. (Courtesy Mary Stuecher)

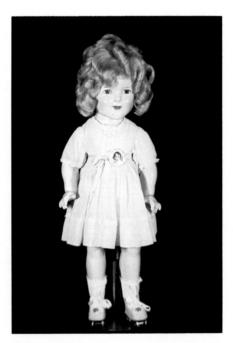

18" All composition and original with rayon tag. Marks: #2/18, on head. #1, on back. Seen in this longer style dress in John Plain catalog. 1940.

22" All composition in Shirley Temple tagged velvet coat and hat worn for American Legion Honorary Member Ceremony. Marks: #2, on head. #4, on body. (Courtesy Mary Stuecher)

18" Marama Doll. All composition with golden brown complexion, brown painted side glancing eyes, glued on black yarn hair, painted mouth and teeth. From movie "Hurricane." Marks: Shirley Temple, on back. This doll was made from Shirley mold by Ideal but it does not represent Shirley in a movie role. (Courtesy Dorothy Cassidy)

16" All composition. Replaced wig. Sunsuit and hat are copies of originals that came with a trunk. Marks: #2, on head #3, on back. (Courtesy Mary Stuecher)

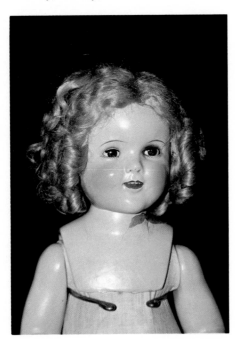

22" Shirley Temple. Composition swivel head on shoulder plate. Cloth body with composition limbs. Hazel sleep eyes/lashes and eyeshadow. Open mouth with six teeth. Rosy blush on hands and knees. Glued on red-blonde wig. Deep dimples. Marks: 20/#2, on head. (Courtesy Mary Stuecher)

Shows full view of cloth body Shirley.

27" All composition mechanical store display Shirley Temple that is fully marked. She has "fixed" one piece body and right leg. Motor is in stand. Originally held her dress tied to arms. (Courtesy Dorothy Cassidy)

Shows full "swing" position of 27" mechanical Shirley Temple.

This is the Mechanical Shirley at the organ. The body and legs are cloth, composition head and arms. Rods attached to keyboard and motor driven to make arms move across keyboard (no music box). The doll would be 15" tall. This item was made and sold by Herbert O. Brown, Fairfield, Maine in 1936. It was actually used by a Broadway Theater in the lobby. (Courtesy Dorothy Cassidy)

Shows profile view of doll at the organ.

11" and 18" Snow White. Of Shirley doll molds but not made to represent her. Mark 18"; #3/18, on back. 11": #1/11. Neither are marked on head.

20" All composition and all original "Littlest Rebel." 1935. Rayon tag. Marks: #2 with 20 reversed and backward, on head. #1/20, on back. Designed by Mollye.

The costumes made for the Ideal vinyl dolls from 1957 through 1974 are too numerous to show. All are tagged, except the last "movie" outfits which have a paper tag "Hong Kong." 12" vinyl and all original with box, tag, purse and pin. 1961.

15" vinyl 1960 all original "Heidi"

15" Vinyl. All original as "Heidi." 1959. This dress and variations of it were also used on the Ideal "Toni" doll.

35" Vinyl. All original. Nylon dress. With original box. Given to Judy Meisinger Christmas, 1960. These dolls identical to Patti Playpal except have jointed wrists.

15" All original. All vinyl. 1958.

15" Vinyl all original "Wee Willie Winkie" 1959.

12" Was originally sold with just slip. 1958.

15" Vinyls with original dresses of differet colors. 1959.

12" Vinyls. Original dresses of different colors. 1959.

12" All vinyl and original as "Capt. January" 1958.

12" Vinyls. 1958 original outfits. Right one is "Rebecca of Sunnybrook Farm."

15" Vinyls. All original as "Heidi" 2 versions. 1961.

12" Vinyl 1960. Original outfits. Left shoes replaced.

12" Vinyl. All original velveteen dresses. 1959. Replaced shoes.

12" Vinyl. Heidi outfits. Replaced shoes. 1959.

15" All vinyl. All original. 1961.

35" Vinyl. Does not have jointed wrists so
may have been a "put together" such as
those sold by Dollspart Co. Sailor top is
original 30's little girl blouse with Shirley
Temple tag. Rest of outfit was Marge' son,
Derryl's. 1960.

16" Vinyl. 1973. All original.

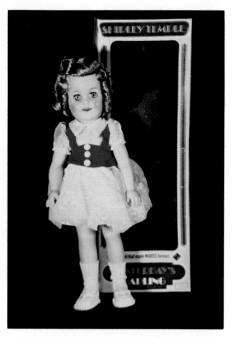

15" 1972 Montgomery Ward Shirley Temple doll. All original.

Store display card for the 16" doll. 1974.

This shows three original Shirleys. First is the latest 1973 vinyl. Middle is 18" and one of the first of composition 1934 with the woven NRA tag. The last is 17" and an early one with the rayon tag.

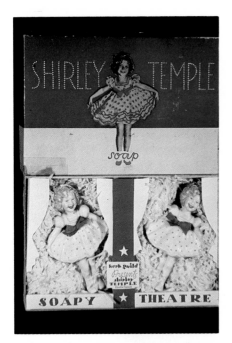

5" Soap Shirley's in original box. "Kerk Guild Soapy Theatre."

Soap figure made from old candy mold. 4½" tall.

5" "soap" figure in original box. By Kerk Guild Inc. Marked: "Shirley Temple on Parade" (Courtesy Mary Stuecher)

All original Shirley Temple charm bracelet from about 1936.

7" Recent (exact age unknown) ceramic figure. Unsigned.

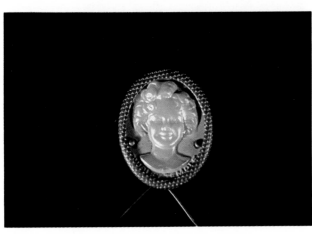

Cameo type. May have originally been on a purse or barrette. Ca. 1930's.

Shows three Shirley Temple doll pins of
the 1930's.

Shows a portion of the jewelry items of
the Marge Meisinger collection.

Original charms with glass enamel. About 1936. The one of Shirley holding dress out is also made in blue.

1¾" original enameled pin of 1930's.

Three recent watches.

Recent "Shrink-Art" Shirley and name pin.

Original jewelry on card. 1961. Given Judy Meisinger as gift. See following photo for detail.

Close up of detail on jewelry on card. No maker identification.

Bronze and silver CERES medals. 1975.

Aluminum and gold CERES medals. 1975. Issued by Food and Agriculture Organization of the United Nations.

Picture pins and locket. None old.

Shows 2 celluloid pins and the larger item is a celluloid mirror. All are from the 1930's.

Close up of undated pin. (Courtesy Dorothy Cassidy)

3 mirrors with celluloid frames. One from 1940's and two from 1930's.

Nanette taffeta dress of the 1930's.

Nanette dress of the 1930's.

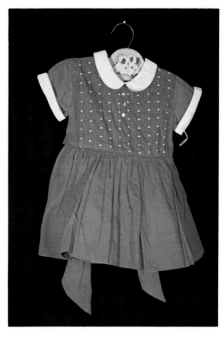

Dress by Nanette Mfg. Co. About 1960.

Cinderella dress of 1960.

Cinderella dress by Roseman Bros. Phila. Pa. of about 1960.

Two dresses by Cinderella. Made by Roseman Bros. Phila. Pa. About 1960.

Cinderella dress of 1960. Made by Roseman Bros. Phila. Pa.

Trimfit socks box. 1930's.

Two Shirley Temple handkerchiefs. These were originally in boxed sets. 1930's.

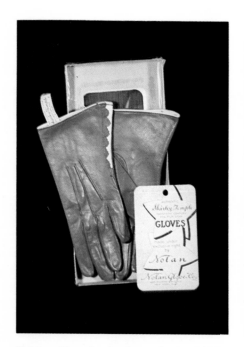

Shirley Temple leather gloves of the 1930's by Nolan Glove Co.

Two Shirley Temple purses with purse mirror and paper tag. By Pyramid. 1930's.

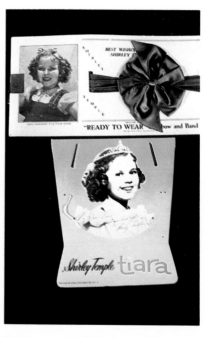

Hairbow card of the late 1930's and Tiara card of 1961.

Shows the original ads along with the bowls, glasses and pitchers by General Mills. These were never given as a set.

Two different pitchers. The taller one is rare and the other is rather common. 1938. These were not given in sets.

Pink plastic tea set of 1959. These also came in larger sets.

Top to box that holds the 1959 plastic tea set.

Shirley Temple Sweet Peas introduced in 1936 and available until recently. Shirley also had a gladiolia, dahlia and daffodil named for her. The Shirley Poppy was not named for her as it was introduced before she was born.

Shows front of box for TV Theatre. 1959.

Shows theatre before "curtain" is up.

6 examples of Shirley Temple Playing Cards by U.S. Playing Card Co. Picture on box matches the backs of the cards.

Shows one of the scenes for the TV Theatre.

Sewing cards #1721. 1936 by Saalfield.

Stationery boxes. 1936. By W.T. & S. Corp. These had a thick cardboard cutout figure of Shirley on top. Stationery is plain.

Composition books and tablets of the 1930's.

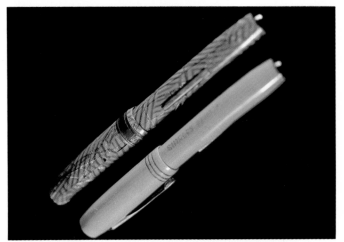

Fountain pens by Eversharp (there were pencils to match). Has Shirley's name on the barrels. 1930's.

"Work With Yarn" box. #1750. By Saalfield. 1936.

Shirley Temple Treasure Board #8806. 1959 by Saalfield.

The Meisingers have hundreds of magazines with Shirley Temple in the contents and over 200 with Shirley on the covers.

Assortment with Shirley covers: Modern Women 1934 (Distributed by the ice companies), Picture Show (British) Dec. 28, 1935, Parents, Oct. 1938. Photoplayer (British) Dec. 28, 1935.

Movie Magazines: Photoplay, Jan. 1935 (Shirley's first and prettiest Photoplay cover). Movie Mirror, Dec. 1934. True Story, Apr. 1936. Movie Mirror, May 1936 (Shirley's Birthday Edition)

Sample Covers for movie magazines. 1930's.

Newspaper TV Sections and TV Guides. Top left from 1970's, others from 1958-60.

Some magazines with Shirley on the covers: Home Movies, Dec. 1939. Dog Craft, Dec. 1938. Current Events, July 31, 1936 and Gentlewomen, Oct. 1934.

Display poster for advertising Nanette clothes. (Courtesy Dorothy Cassidy)

Movie lobby display from the Royal Oak Theatre, Mich. Measures 6 feet by 3½ feet. Ad for movie "Little Miss Marker." (Courtesy Mary Stuecher)

Left: From a large size portfolio of drawings of stars done in Australia. "The Dality" New Year Edition, Jan. 1, 1937. Right: Lobby photo. Shirley's picture on both sides of cardboard.

Newspaper Magazine Sections: Screen and Radio Weekly, Nov. 29, 1936. This Week, May 5, 1935.

Midweek Pictorial, Jan. 5, 1935 and Picture Show (British), Apr. 16, 1938.

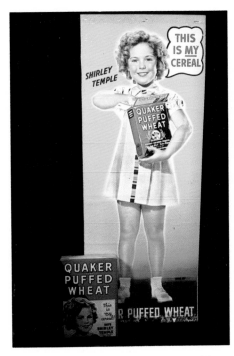

Old poster with Puffed Wheat box. About 1937. Shirley also appeared in ads for Wheaties, Bisquick, Drifted Snow Flour, Florists Telegraph Delivery, Teledial Radios, Dodge cars, Lane Cedar Chests, Woodbury's Face Powder, Royal Crown Cola, Calox Tooth Powder, Oneida Silverware, Lux Toilet Soap, Deltab Simulated Pearls, KM Appliances, V-8 Juice, and many others.

Lobby Stills and Lobby Cards. 1930's.

6 of set of 12 (No. 1-6) Wheaties pix. 1936.

6 of set of 12 (No. 7-12) Wheaties pix. 1936.

Set #2112 by Saalfield. 1934. Shows one of the four dolls from this set. (Courtesy Mary Stuecher)

This is a framed and dressed paper-doll of the 1930's.

Set #2112 by Saalfield. 1934. There are four dolls in the set. Each are 8" tall. This was the very first of many paperdolls issued. (Courtesy Mary Stuecher)

Shirley Temple statuette doll by Saalfield. 1935. Doll is 8" tall. (Courtesy Mary Stuecher)

9½" Small doll on back cover of "Shirley Temple, A Life Like Paper Doll." 1936 by Saalfield. (Courtesy Mary Stuecher)

Boxed Playhouse Set includes standing paperdoll #1739. Saalfield. 1935.

Shows 16" paperdoll (standing) from what set and date is unknown. (Courtesy Dorothy Cassidy)

"Shirley Temple Dolls and Dresses" #1761 Saalfield 1937. Two 14½" tall dolls with authentic personal and movie wardrobe. (Courtesy Mary Stuecher)

Paper clothes from Saalfield set #1761. (Courtesy Mary Stuecher)

Shows second paperdoll that is in set #1761. (Courtesy Mary Stuecher)

Clothes from set #1761 Saalfield. 1937. (Courtesy Mary Stuecher)

Saalfield's set #1761. 1937. (Courtesy Mary Stuecher)

Additional clothes from Saalfield set #1761 (Courtesy Mary Stuecher)

Top: #303 Saalfield 1937. #1787 Saalfield 1940. Lower: Spanish paper dolls.

Cover of Saalfield's 1942 book #2425. Has set of two 10½" dolls with teenage movie and personal wardrobe. (Courtesy Mary Stuecher)

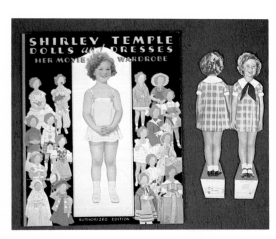

Shirley Temple dolls and dresses with movie wardrobe. 1938 by Saalfield. Shirley Temple figurette—a giveaway. 1935.

Second and back cover doll from Saalfield set #2425. (Courtesy Mary Stuecher)

Paper doll over 2 feet high. #300 by Gabriel. 1958.

Top: 18" standing doll #1348. Saalfield
1959 No. 4435. Saalfield 1958. Lower:
(Same doll as #1348, only thicker) #5110
Saalfield and #1715 by Saalfield. 1935.

Jack and Jill paperdoll reprint of 1934 set.
May 1959.

Top: #1725 Saalfield 1960. #1789 Saalfield
1960. Lower: #2425 Saalfield 1942. #2112
Saalfield 1934.

Paperdolls by modern artists Emma Terry and Marilyn Henry.

Paper dolls by modern artist Emma
Terry.

#1768. 1937 by Saalfield.

Book #1772 by Saalfield. 1937.

Top: Saalfield 1935 and #1554 by Saalfield. 1958. Lower: Saalfield #1654. 1958 and Dell Pub. Co. 1935 Birthday Book with paperdoll.

Shows front and back of book #1711. 1936 by Saalfield.

Left: #1717. 1936 by Saalfield. Right: #1784 By Saalfield 1939.

Top: Movieland Wax Museum. Apco Pub. Co. 1966 Saalfield #4884. 1959. Lower: #5653 by Saalfield 1959 and #4624, Saalfield. 1959.

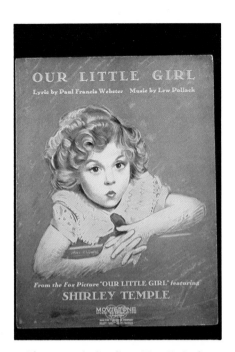

Sheet music by Sam Fox Pub Co. 1935.

Sheet music by Sam Fox Pub. Co. 1936.

Top: Hollywood Dance Folio #16. 1937 by Robbins Music Corp. Album by Sam Fox Pub. Co. 1957. Lower: Album by Sam Fox 1935 (reissued 1960's). Favorite Songs. 1937 by Robbins Music Corp.

Song Albums: Left: French by Sam Fox 1934. Beautiful color plates and drawings. Right: 1936 by Sam Fox Pub. Co.

Sheet music: Top: Sam Fox Pub. Co. 1935 (both). Lower: Irving Caesar, Inc. 1936. Sam Fox Pub. Co. 1937.

Sheet music. Top: Robbins Music Corp. 1940. Crawford Music Corp. 1943. Lower: Williamson Music Corp. 1943. Paul-Pioneer Music Corp. 1947.

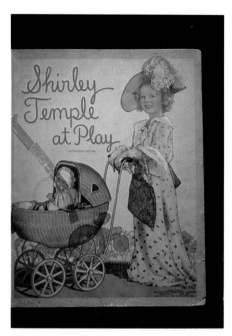

"Shirley Temple At Play" by Saalfield. #1712. 1935.

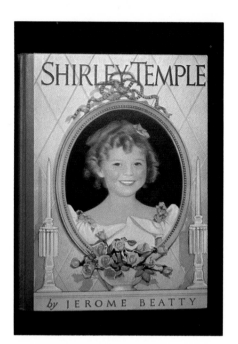

"Shirley Temple" by Jerome Beatty. 1935 by Saalfield. Two versions of book found. Identical except last few pages updated to include latest movie. (Courtesy Mary Stuecher)

Phonograph records: Left: 20th Cent. Fox #3006. 1958. 1 record. Right: 20th Cent. Fox #FEP 100. 1958. 1 record.

Four issues of Bambi: All by RCA Victor. Top: #LBY1012. 1 record. #Y395. About 1945. 3-10" 78RPM records. Lower: #EP. 1949. #WY391. 1949. 2 records and booklet of pictures.

Phonograph records. Top: 20th Cent. Fox (Made in England) 1974. 1 record. Music For Pleasure (England) #MFP 1141. 1967 1 record. Lower: Starline (England) #MRS5085. 1971. 1 record. Golden Record EP602. 1962. Shirley songs but not sung by her.

Hard covers. Top: Little Colonel. Johnston Bust & Co. 1935. Heidi. Saalfield. 1937. Came in red and blue covers. Blue slightly larger. Lower: Poems #1720. Saalfield. 1936.

Big little books by Saalfield. Top: Littlest Rebel. Hard cover #1115. 1935. My Life and Times #1116. 1936. Story of Shirley Temple. Hard cover. #1089. 1934. Lower: Littlest Rebel. Soft cover. #1595. 1935. Story of Shirley Temple. Soft cover #1319. 1934. Little Colonel #1095. 1935.

All Saalfield and soft covers: I Am Eight #1776. 1937. Little Star. #1762. 1936. Dimples. #1760. 1936. Stowaway. #1767. 1937.

All Saalfield and soft covers: Little Miss #1778. 1938. Susannah #1785. 1939. Little Princess #1783. 1939. Wee Willie Winkie. #1789. 1937.

All hard covers, but last one. My Young Life. Garden City Pub. Co. 1945. Spirit of Dragonwyck. 1945 by Kathryn Heisenfelt. Whitman. Screaming Spector. 1946 by Kathryn Heisenfelt. Whitman. Honeymoon (paperback) Bart House #103. 1947.

Treasury books. Random House 1959. Heidi Xl, Littlest Rebel X2, Rebecca of Sunnybrook Farm X3, Susannah of the Mounties X4, Capt. January and Little Colonel X5.

Top: Random House. 1958. Paperback by Lois Ely Monarch book K62. 1962. Lower: Random House. 1958.

Top: Random House 1958. Random House 1961. Lower: Random House 1962. Random House 1958.

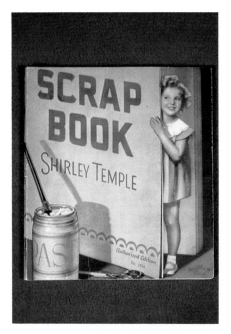

Scrapbook #1714. 1935 by Saalfield.   Scrapbook #1722. 1936 by Saalfield.   Scrapbook #1763. 1937 by Saalfield.

Shirley Temple 16MM Safety Films by Keystone Mfg. Co. 1930's. 100 feet of film in original box. (Courtesy Mary Stuecher)

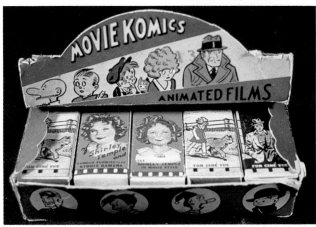

Movie Komics Animated Films. Pathe Laboratories. 1935. For use with Kiddie Kamera.

Top: Keystone Mfg. Co. 16MM "Shirley's Bedtime" 1930's. Pathegram #609 "Shirley Temple" 1930's. Lower: Allied Mfg. "Shirley Temple" 1940's.

49

Ken Films. Recent packaging of old films.
Mostly 8MM.

Souvenir books from Tournament of
Roses. Shirley Temple was Grand Marshall in 1939. The youngest to this day
ever to be accorded this honor. Left: 1975
book. Right: Two different booklets of
1939.

Cotton material and wrapping paper. Late
1960's.

Top: Tablet 1962 by Western Tablets.
Advertisitng fan for Royal Crown Cola
about 1943. Lower: 1950 Movie Star
Calender. Shirley is on October page.

Spanish cigar band of the 1930's.

"Little Miss" sewing machine. Not authentic but definitely copying Shirley Temple. 1936.

1930's string holder of plastic. String comes through the mouth.

Stamps from British Movie mag. 1930's. Stars stamp 1940's. Gummed picture stamp and band from Trimfit socks. 1930's.

Top: Shirley Temple Pencil Box. Lower: Shirley Temple paper mask. Supposed to be from Chicago World's Fair, also N.Y. Macy's Store.

Giveaway booklet by various merchants advertising their products as well as the movie "Curly Top" 1935. Very cute little booklet and story.

Small flip booklet. 32 pages. About 1935.

Shirley Temple's Book of Fairy Tales published by The Saalfield Publishing Co. Akron, Ohio. Copyright 1936, although the basic book without the Shirley pictures was copyrighted in 1922. This book contains many unusual pictures of Shirley with animals.

Inside cover of the Shirley Temple Book of Fairy Tales.

52

All by Saalfield and soft cover: Play #1712. 1935. Poor Little Rich Girl #1723. 1936. How I Raised #945. 1935 (From Silver Screen Mag) Through the Day. #1716. 1936.

Boxed set #1730. Saalfield. 1936.

Shirley Temple is on the cover of this book titled "Stars and Films of 1937" by Daily Express Publications. Edited by Stephen Watts.

All Saalfield and soft covers: Little Girl #1775. 1938. Heidi #337. 1937. (Black and white). Heidi #1771. 1937. Her Life #1734. 1938.

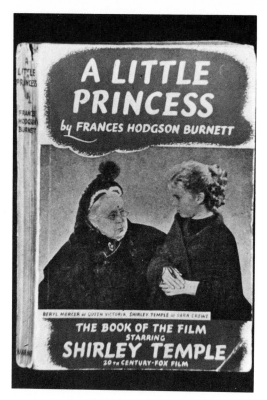

All hard covers. Top: Shirley Temple Annual. Daily Herald Ltd. London. 1930's. Petite Princesse. Hachette. France. 1939. Lower: All by Saalfield. Pastime #1726. 1935. Story Book #1726. 1935. Has paperdoll reproduction of "Playhouse" kit. Shirley Temple by Jerome Beaty #1737.

The Little Princess by Fredrick Warne and Co. Ltd. London and New York. No date but from about 1939.

Germany program and story book of Shirley Temple in "The Little Princess." 1939.

A fine reference book on Shirley Temple by Jeanine Basinger. Editor: Ted Sennett and published by Pyramid Publications, New York.

One of the most helpful reference to the life and dates, a book by renown authority on Shirley Temple, Loraine Burdick. Published by Jonathan David, Middle Village, N.Y. 11379.

Current books that include Shirley Temple. "Fox Girls" is excellent.

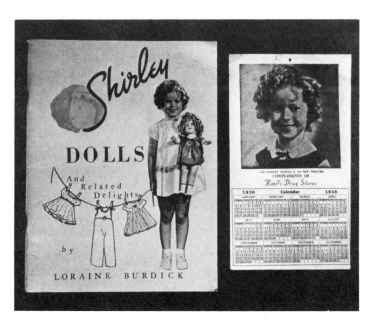

Left: Loraine Burdick. Quest books 1966. A wonderful book of Shirley collectibles and information. Right: Calendar 1936.

Four booklets by Loraine Burdick. Quest Books. 1973. Cute photos.

Shirley Temple wood buggy. Has Shirley decal on each side, also hubcaps say "Shirley Temple" as also do the two side knobs at the base of the hood. This buggy is 32" high and 29" long. Made by F.A. Whitney Carriage Co. These buggies came in grey, black and a dark blue which was sold by Sears, Roebuck.

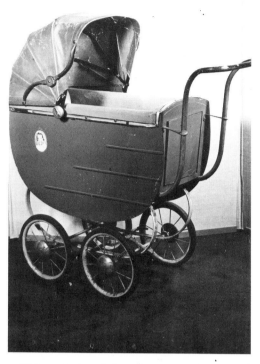

This variation of the Whitney buggy is 34" high and 34½" long. Shirley Temple Doll buggies were also made in wicker.

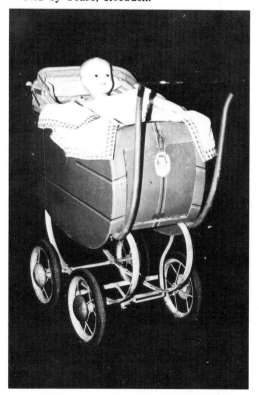

Shirley Temple Doll Buggy. Shirley emblem on front of buggy. "Shirley Temple" on hubcaps. Made by F.A. Whitney Carriage Co. Leominster, Mass. (Courtesy Pauline Minnick Collection)

This wicker Shirley Temple buggy is rarer than the others. (Courtesy Sandy Crump)

McCall pattern #525. Copyright 1937. Original marked price is 25 cents. (Courtesy Mary Stuecher)

McCall pattern #418. Copyright 1938. Original price was 25 cents. (Courtesy Mary Stuecher)

Original hairbow card of the 1930's.

3 hairbows with "cameo" of Shirley. 1930's. Pale blue, dark blue and white.

Shirley Temple Slippers box by Restful. 1930's.

Trimfit socks. 1958.

Pale blue/white pinafore Nanette Mfg. Co. dress of about 1960.

Dress tag for Nanette dress of 1930's.

Nanette dress tag of the 1930's.

Nanette dress tag of the 1930's.

Dress tag for Nanette fashions of about 1960.

Dress tag by Cinderella of about 1960.

Glove tag of 1930's by Nolan Glove Co.

Purse tag of 1930's by Pyramid Co.

Recent T-Shirt from Stars Hall of Fame, Florida.

Recent blouse with movie star pictures, including Shirley Temple.

Recent T-Shirt

59

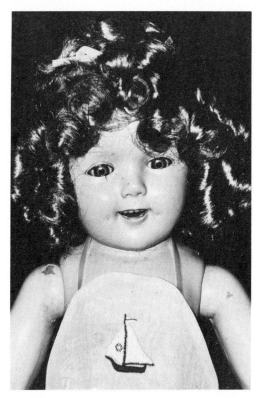

27" All composition. Green tin sleep eyes, lashes. Open mouth with six teeth. Dimples. Replaced wig. Wears copy of sunsuit from trunk set. Marks: #2, on head. Backwards 27/Ideal Doll/Made in USA, on back. (Courtesy Mary Stuecher)

18" All composition. Original clothes from the "Bluebird." Marks: Shirley Temple, on head. U.S.A./Shirley Temple/18, on body. (Courtesy Mandeville-Barkel Collection)

13" All composition with flirty eyes. All original. This doll called the Lucky Penny Doll for her role in "Just Around the Corner." Marks: Shirley Temple, on head. Shirley Temple/13, on back. Tag: Genuine Shirley Temple/Doll, etc. (Courtesy Mandeville-Barkel Collection)

13" All composition and original in trunk with wardrobe. (Courtesy Mandeville-Barkel Collection)

19" Vinyl with flirty eyes. Replaced wig. All original. Pale yellow with black trim. 1957.

17" All original. 19" with flirty eyes. Both are vinyl. White with red trim. 1959.

19" All original. Both are vinyl. 17" wears part of the "Wee Willie Winkie" outfit. Red plaid/green vest.

Two 15" Vinyl. Original. Left: pale blue. Right: white with blue skirt with red/ white and blue trim. 1960.

15" and 17" All vinyl 1960. Original blue coats.

15" Vinyls. Original except shoes on left. Left doll is dressed as "Poor Little Rich Girl" in blue and white trim. Right is "Heidi" in red/green and white. 1960.

15" Vinyl. All original. 1961. Blue top with white trim and white skirt with blue trim.

36" All vinyl with rooted hair. All original. Marks: Ideal Doll/ST-35-38-2, on head. Ideal Toy Corp./6-35-7, on body. (Courtesy Mandeville-Barkel Collection)

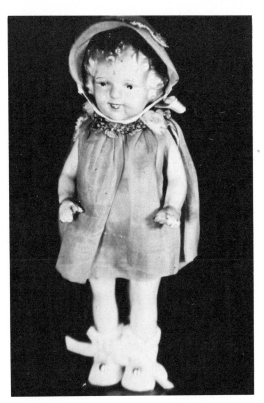

7½" Composition. No mark. Believed to be made in Japan. Jointed shoulders and hips only.

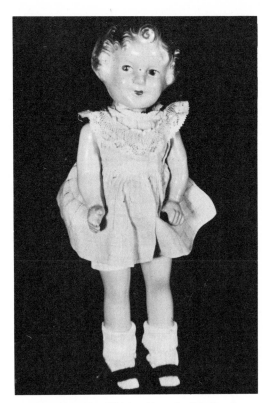

9" Composition Shirley Temple. Marks: 9/Ideal/Doll.

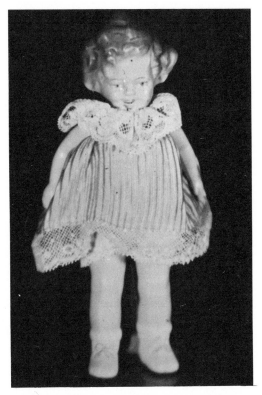

6½" Bisque. Marked Made in Japan. Jointed shoulders and hips only. Painted on shoes/socks.

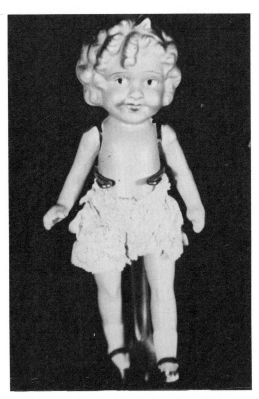

6½" Bisque. Replaced arms. No marks. Believed to be made in Japan.

4" Bisque. Marked Germany. Fully jointed. Painted on shoes.

Recent 16" bisque Shirley Temple. Made from the composition molding. Wearing 1934 doll dress.

13" Recent bisque Shirley Temple

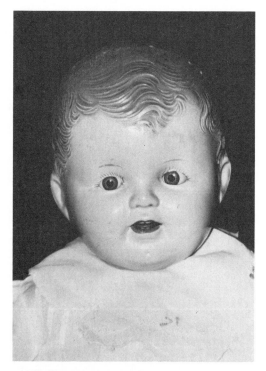

23" Composition swivel head on rubber shoulder plate, cloth body, rubber arms, composition legs, grey tin flirty sleep eyes, no lashes. Open mouth with two upper and two lower teeth. Molded, painted orange hair. Three dimples. Marks: In. & T. Co. Although body is identical to Shirley baby doll, this is not a Shirley baby. (Courtesy Mary Stuecher)

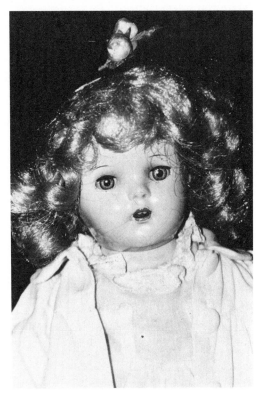

13" All composition made from the Shirley Temple mold. Blue tin sleep eyes, open mouth with four teeth. Glued on very curly blonde wig. Old, but not original clothes. Marks: Rubbed out Shirley Temple/13 on back. (Courtesy Mary Stuecher)

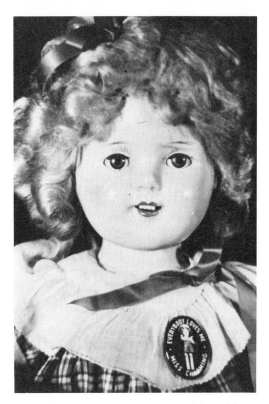

18" "Miss Charming" all composition. All original including pin. Made by Goldberger Co. (Eegee) and marked E.G., on head.

This pin goes with a Goldberger (Eegee) doll that is like Miss Charming and a Shirley Temple look-a-like. The pin says "Little Miss Movie."

19" "Nancy" All composition and all original Shirley Temple look-a-like designed by same designer, Bernard Lipfert. This doll was advertised as "The Movie Queen." By Arranbee Doll Co.

20" Shirley Temple look-a-like. Composition shoulder head and limbs. Blue tin sleep eyes. Glued on blonde mohair wig, open mouth with five teeth. No dimples. Marks: none. Costume is copy of "Stowaway" outfit. (Courtesy Mary Stuecher)

17" Shirley Temple look-a-like. All composition with blue-green tin sleep eyes, open mouth with six teeth. Glued on blonde mohair wig, chin dimple. Marks: none. All original costume. (Courtesy Mary Stuecher)

18" All composition. Body made from Shirley Temple mold with Patsy type face. Blue sleep eyes with lashes. Blonde human hair wig over molded Patsy type hair. Dress from 1930's but not original to doll. Marks: Shirley Temple/18, on body. (Courtesy Mary Stuecher)

19" Shirley Temple look-alike. All composition with brown tin sleep eyes/lashes. Open mouth with four teeth. Glued blonde mohair wig. Dimples. Marks: none. Costume is copy of "Our Little Girl" outfit. (Courtesy Mary Stuecher)

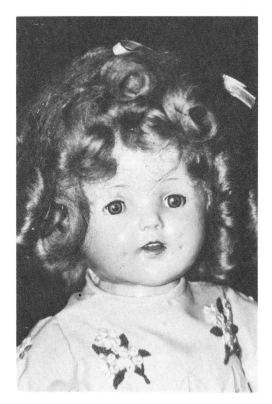

16" Shirley Temple look-a-like. All composition with blue tin sleep eyes/lashes. Open mouth with four teeth. Replaced wig. 3 dimples (2 in one cheek). Marks: none. Costume is copy of "Curly Top" daisy dress. (Courtesy Mary Stuecher)

18" Shirley Temple look-a-like. All composition with Patsy type body. Glued on blonde mohair wig, deep blue sleep eyes/lashes. Open mouth with six teeth. No dimples. Marks: none. All original costume. (Courtesy Mary Stuecher)

17" All vinyl re-issues of 1972. Marks: 1972 Ideal Toy Corp./ST-14-H-213, on head. 1971/Ideal Toy Corp. /ST-14-b-38, on body. Top row: Rebecca, Little Colonel & Capt. January. Lower row: Original issue, Heidi. The four movie outfits were sold separately. (Courtesy Mandeville-Barkel Collection.

18" Cinderella. All composition. Flirty green eyes. Eyeshadow/lashes and painted lashes below the eyes. Open mouth with four teeth. All original. Marks: Shirley Temple (straight)/18, on back. Dimple in chin only.

14½" Bright Star (Shirley Temple look-a-like) by Horsman Dolls, Inc. All composition. Blue tin sleep eyes, four teeth and metal tongue. Golden blonde mohair wig. No marks on doll. Paper tag on dress: Horsman's Bright Star/with eyes that shine/and hair so fine. Tag on underclothes: Regal Doll Corporation/Horsman Dolls, Trenton, N.J./Style No. 526. Original. (Courtesy John Axe)

19" "Little Miss Movie Star." All vinyl with softer vinyl head. Eyes are rounder and teeth are formed as part of the mouth with the teeth area painted. Marks: 19/S/AE/195. Maker unknown. (Courtesy John Axe)

Shows full view of the 1957(/) Shirley Temple copy.

This is an ad picture of the original Shirley Temple Ranger doll or cowgirl doll which came in three sizes only: 27", 17" and 11".

This shows the ad contained in the Film Pictorial, England of Aug. 1, 1936. The dolls are all felt like cloth with face "Masks" painted with oil paints.

Full page ad of 1935. The Shirley Temple dolls were offered through many newspapers and magazines.

Ad in a 1956-7-or8 catalog (material undated) Shows a "copy" of Shirley Temple. Doll is all vinyl. See doll on page 68.

Mollye fashioned red velvet coat and hat. (Courtesy Shirley Bertrand)

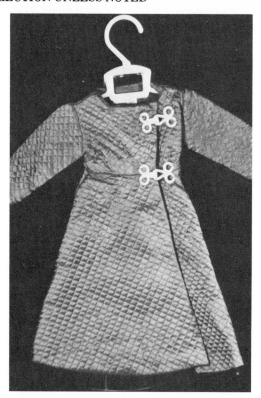

Mollye fashioned red robe for the Shirley Temple doll. (Courtesy Shirley Bertrand)

Fashion designed and made by Mollye for the Shirley Temple doll. Rose coat and hat with dark blue plaid. (Courtesy Shirley Bertrand)

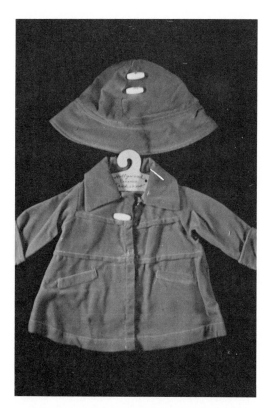

This is a Mollye Goldman designed and sold velvet coat and tam for the Shirley Temple doll. The top of the box is one of the "give-a-way" photos of Shirley and the box end reads: "Genuine Shirley Temple Doll Outfit No. 22-90. Reg. Trademark. Made in U.S.A.

This is an early Molly tag on doll clothes.

This is box that held extra doll clothes.
1930's. Blue background and pink dress.

Box for extra doll clothes. 1930's.

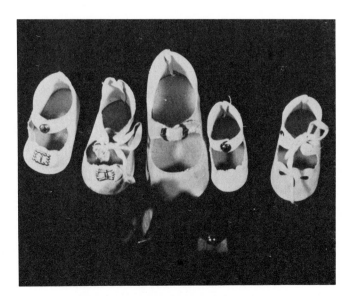

Different versions of original shoes for the
composition Shirley Temple dolls.

Shoes and socks in accessories box for 12".
Late 1950's.

1930's shoes and socks with blue/pink
roses shoebag in original box.

Wooden rack for doll clothes. Believe it
was on a stand. 1930's.

1930's light blue cardboard doll clothes
hanger.

Red shoes manufactured by Premier for
12" Shirley (They could not use "Temple")
Late 1950's.

Patterns for doll clothes of 1930's except
upper left and lower right, from the
1950's.

Patterns for Shirley Temple doll clothes.
1930's except lower left, which is copy
from 1950's.

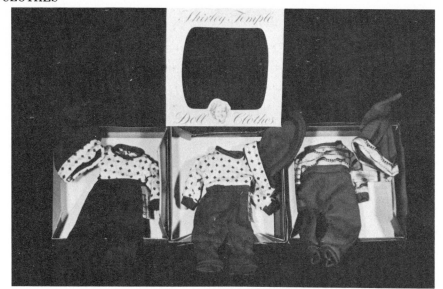

3 versions of pajamas in original boxes. 12". 1959. Left is blue, center, red and right red and yellow.

2 versions of raincoats in original boxes. 12". Right: Teal blue, 1959. Left: White, 1960.

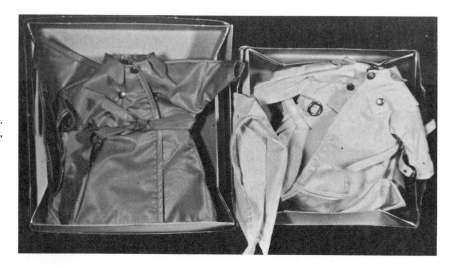

Dresses made by Premier for 17" and 12" Shirley. Late 1950's. Left is blue and right, pink.

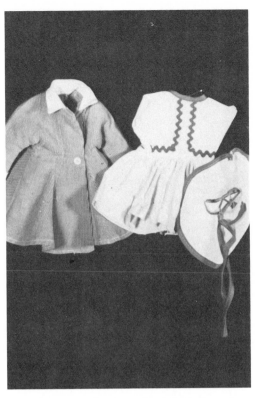

2 original outfits for 12", 1960. Left: pale yellow/red trim. Coat is mustard with white trim.

3 original rayon fleece coats for 12" about 1960. Red, yellow and green.

Embroidered pot holder 5" square. Ca. 1930's. There were many items including dresser scarves and chair backs. (Courtesy Mary Stuecher)

Embroidery set #310. 1959 by Gabriel.

Movie Favorites Embroidery set #301. By Gabriel about 1960.

1960 Gabriel embroidery set #311.

Shows 2 pins from Shirley Temple's 1967 political campaign. The picture is from the 1950's.

Items from Shirley Temple Black political campaign. 1967.

4½" "salt" figures. Ca. 1935.

3 different figures. 2 outside ones are "salt" and rose color. The middle is off white and recent stonelike material made in Greece. Flocked dress also came in red.

3 ¾" silver and gold caricature plaster statues. Ca. 1930's.

13" Composition statue of Shirley Temple. The dress and base are painted pale green. Eyes are painted brown. (Courtesy Kay Bransky)

7" Pale blue hand painted plaster with glazed finish. 1960's. (Courtesy Mary Stuecher)

7" Plaster figurine. Date and maker unknown.

12" Carnival plaster Shirley of the 1930's.
(Courtesy Sandy Crump)

12" Carnival plaster figure of 1930's. Re-painted.

Shirley Temple Beauty Bar, #341 by Gabriel. 1959.

Shirley Temple Glamour Bar #450 by Gabriel. 1962. Includes all items listed on box.

79

Cloisonne silver bracelet from Denmark.
1936.

These gold color charms are from 1936.

Necklace and bracelet set. In original box.
1936.

This pin was from the 1936 Chicago Times Shirley Temple Club. See Photo section for the give-a-way picture that went with this pin.

Picture rings believed to be from the 1930's.

Close up of 1930's ring. (Courtesy Dorothy Cassidy)

Silver pin from Netherlands Shirley Temple Club. 1937. About ¾" in diameter.

Gold 3 pieces of jewelry. Dates unknown.

Recent Movieland Wax Museum Charm and a recent photo charm.

All these items are recent.

Two recent pins from the Stars Hall of Fame, Florida.

Recent mirrors and doll pin.

These are all recent doll pins.

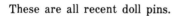

Recent bisque Shirley Temple pin.

German Periodical of 1930's. "Das Schwal-
bchen" which translated is: The Little
Swallow. Periodical for home and family.
99th issue, third year. Cover phot titled
"Unser Engelchen." Translated is "Our
Little Angel." (Courtesy Mary Stuecher)

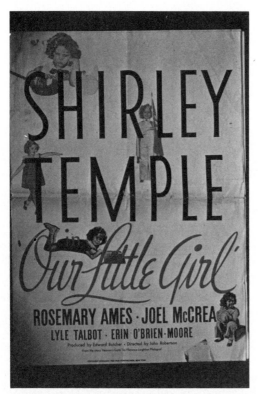

Shirley Temple paperweight believed to
be of recent vintage using old paperweight and a Shirley Temple playing card.

Pressbook for "Our Girl Shirley." 1934.

Magazine of the California Zoological Society with Shirley's picture on the back cover. The dog in the picture is named Rowdy.

Style Parade and Recipe Book for 1935 featured movie stars throughout and was sold for $1.00 at movie theatres. There was one put out in 1936 also.

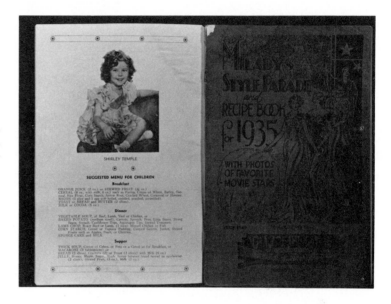

Aug. 1, 1936 issue of Film Pictorial, England which not only included the special section but the photo shown in the following picture.

Give-a-way photo by the Film Pictorial,
England on Aug. 1, 1936.

FAO Schwarz "Toys Through The Years"
Text by Marvin Schwarz. Doubleday &
Co. Inc. 1975. Picture of Shirley Temple
doll on cover only.

Newspaper T.V. Sections. First one from
1970's, other two from 1958.

The April, 1949 Shirley Temple 21st
birthday album by Dell.

Shirley Temple's Magnetic T.V. Theater. Has many scene changes and figures. Magnets under the floor change the position of the figures. Metal base is marked: American Metal Specalties Corp.

This is the box top that contains the Shirley Temple Theater.

Shows letter to children from Shirley Temple.

1 ¾" long Shirley Temple Police badge. Good quality bronze. Marks: A. Stamp & Sty.80/L.A. Cal.

Here Shirley Temple gives her "Shirley Temple Police Badge" to the nations #1 G-Man, J.Edgar Hoover. He in return, gives Shirley his autograph. Dated Sept. 16, 1937.

The Shirley Temple Bath Drum. Contained castile soap with a rope to hang around the neck. Designed by Lester Gaba and made by Kerk Guild. 347 Fifth Ave. New York.

Play Beauty Shop rubber curlers for the Shirley Temple Doll. No manufacture information is listed on the package.

Two recent photo plates.

Sheet music. Both from "Stand Up & Cheer" by Sam Fox Pub. Co. 1934.

Sheet music by Famous Music Corp. 1934.

Sheet music. Sam Fox Pub. Co. 1934.

Sheet music by Sam Fox Pub. Co. 1934.

Sheet music by Robbins Music Corp. 1936.

Sheet music by Leo Feist, Inc. 1936.

Sheet music by Robbins Music Corp. 1936.

Sheet music by Sam Fox Pub. Co. 1935.

Sheet music. Top: Circle Music Pub. Inc.
1938. Crawford Music Corp. 1938. Lower:
Leo Feist, Inc. 1938. Hollywood Songs.
1938.

Sheet music. Top: Robbins Music Corp. 1938. Shows re-issue. Lower: Re-issue. Choral arrangement by Sam Fox Pub. Co. 1935.

Sheet music by Robbins Music Corp. 1936.

Phonograph records. Top: 20th Century Fox #1003. Late 1950's. 1 record. 20th Cent. Fox #TCF1032. Late 1950's. 2 records. Lower: Pickwick International SPC3177. 1970's. 1 record Back view (front same as above) PTP2034. 2 records.

Phonograph records. Top: Movietime MTM 1001. 1965. 1 record. 20th Century Fox. #T906. 1973. 2 records. Lower: Movietime #71012. 1966. 1 record. Walt Disney CAS1026(e). 1960. 1 record.

Phonograph records. Top: 20th Cent. Fox #3006. 1960's. 1 record. 20th Cent. Fox #3045. 1960's. 1 record. Lower: 20th Cent. Fox #TFM3172. 1965. 1 record. 20th Cent. Fox #TFM3102. 1963.

Boxed set with standing doll #1727. Saalfield. 1935.

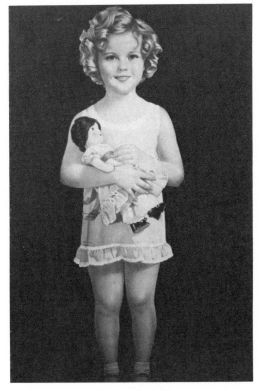

34" paper doll #1765. 1936 by Saalfield.

Outfits for 34" doll. 9" doll included in set.

Shirley Temple Christmas Book with paperdoll. #1770. Saalfield 1937.

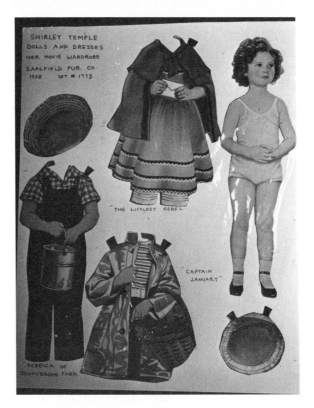

"Shirley Temple Doll & Dresses" by Saalfield 1938. #1773. Set has 2 10" paperdolls. Movie wardrobe. (Courtesy Mary Stuecher)

Additional movie wardrobe from Saalfield set #1773. (Courtesy Mary Stuecher)

Shows the box for the 40" cardboard paperdoll with movie wardrobe. (Courtesy Sandy Crump)

These paperdolls are cut and we have no information on them. They are a really cute and delightful set. Shirley is only one with brown eyes. Ca. 1930's.

Snap on paperdolls. #300. Gabriel 1958.

Shirley Temple Play Kit #9869. 1961 by Saalfield.

Magnetic paperdoll #303 by Gabriel. 1961.   Inside of Play Kit #9869. 1961 Saalfield.

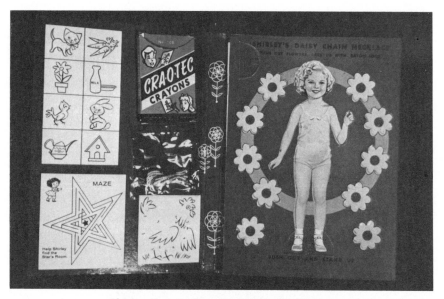

Shirley Temple Play Kit #9869. Saalfield.
1961.

Modern artist, Loraine Wood, paperdolls with joints. 1974. (Courtesy Mary Stuecher)

About a 1935 newspaper doll by Laura Brock.

A gift card with actual signature. 1938.

This is the February 10, 1935 issue cover of the Boston Post, a Valentine from Shirley Temple.

A few of the many foreign film booklets.

Top Birthday card is marked "Buzza Craftacres, Mpls, U.S.A. The lower one is not marked, except with the number 10 B 853. Inside is written 1936.

If These Schools Are Phony—

WHEN National Talent Pictures studios were raided (see page 9), people all over the country decided Hollywood movie schools must be the bunk. Newspapers encouraged that conclusion. SCREEN GUIDE investigated, got the real story. It prints it first, here and now:

One and only one of more than seventy-five schools was at fault. Even in that case the judge who pronounced a verdict of guilty said the school was apparently teaching its pupils well. From this comparatively tiny seed sprang a scandal that encompassed all other movie schools. Never in the history of Hollywood, home of the stony heart and the double-cross, has there been a greater injustice than this heaping of abuse on innocents. While others are content to peddle scandal, SCREEN GUIDE hastens to call attention to this truth—and to place serious blame where it really belongs.

Despite the highly ballyhooed "search for talent" by the studios, there is not one studio-endorsed school to help new-comers prepare themselves. Robert Taylor graduated from a movie school right in Hollywood. So also did Shirley Temple, Jane Withers, June Lang, many others. Disregarding this, studios warn, "Stay away from Hollywood!" But few can believe that success comes to those who dodge it; hopefuls come by thou-

Application enrolling Shirley in the Meglin Dance Studios. Dated 9/17/31. From Screen Guide Dec. 1938. (Courtesy Mary Stuecher)

98

This is a drawing by Shirley Temple in 1937. Almost looks like a "self-portrait."

These labels are made of cardboard and marked: No. 561 Emanuel Heller, Vienna, Austria.

Letter which accompanied the "Movie-ette" flip booklet. See color section under "books."

Movie programs. Each has four pages.

99

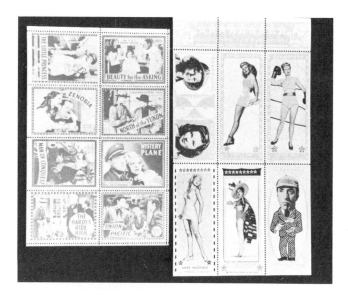

"My Weekly Reader" newspaper used in schools for many years and used Shirley Temple as subject material several times.

A set of stamps that show Shirley Temple in the 1939 movie "The Little Princess." The other shows her as a child and a teenager. "Hollywood Official Stamps of the Stars & Studios—First Series." Dated 1947.

Left: Dollspart catalog page (1960') offering Shirley Temple doll parts for a "put together" doll or for damaged parts. These were also available in the 35" size. Right: Leaflet from Meyer Jacoby Co. 1957 announcing they will sell Shirley Temple dolls. They also handled Shirley Temple wigs and still do.

Top: 1. Part of set of movie star pictures. 1940's. 2. Recent card from set of movie star pictures. 3. Cinderella dress tag of about 1960. Lower: 1. Card of 1950. 2. recent matchbox cover. 3. recent card. 4. 1940's card.

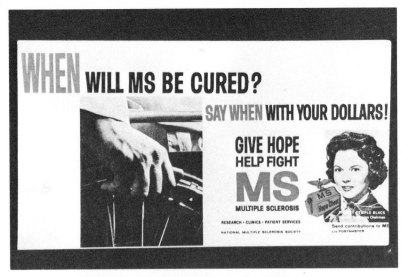

Shirley Temple Black was the National Campaign Chairman for Multiple Sclerosis in 1966.

Three of set of four coloring books #1732. 1937 by Saalfield.

Shirley Temple Bluebird Coloring Book by Saalfield. Date unknown. (Courtesy Mary Stuecher)

#1779. 1939 Saalfield. Lower right: Film Festival book by Baskin-Robbins Ice Cream. 1965. Lower left: #5236. 1959 by Saalfield.

Advertising Poster. 1930's.

Advertising posters of the 1930's.

These are two Life magazine ads of about 1944 or 1945.

Shows an ad for Royal Crown Cola. Ca. 1944.

Lux ad in the Ladies' Home Companion. November 1949.

Packet of Party invitations by Freelance. 1973.

A $10.00 play money bill with Shirley Temple dated 1972 by Wm. E. Beyer Assoc. Inc. The other is a photo of Shirley that is glued to a 1963 "Fowler" dollar bill. Maker unknown.

103

Recent paper tablet.

Shows two current greeting cards. Left is by Freelance, Dansdale, Pa. 19446.

Current Telephone book cover (1975) used in many cities.

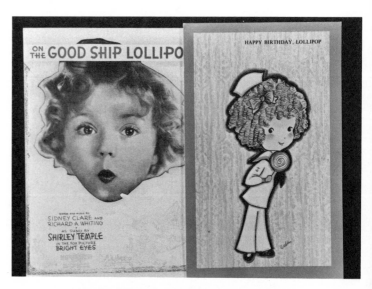

The Good Ship Lollipop card was made by Historical Greeting Cards by Clay, 509 St. Ann, New Orleans. The "Happy Birthday-Lollipop" card was made by Panda Prints Inc. and designed by Rosalind Welcher.

A Toast to Shirley Temple

Your head a dream ship piled with gold,
Such treasure as no pirate knew—
Wind-crumpled gold in living rings
Of light; a favor granted few.

Your laughing eyes imprison gnomes
Of mischief, and the starlight, too;
And in their innocence the world
Of God that all have longed to view.

Your ruddy lips, they shame the rose,
Expressing all you wish them to;
They are fond doors that open wide
When song and gladness ripple through.

Your chubby hands and chubby wrists,
Your feet, that ramble as they do,
The whole sweet bundle that you are
We love, my dear, because it's YOU!

By P. J. CLEVELAND

ILLUSTRATED BY FRANK DOBIAS

Photoplay Jan. 1937

71

The following lists may not be complete but contains all the articles, photos, covers, etc. that are in the Meisinger collection and ones that Marge knows about from information from other Shirley Temple collectors. The notation following each:

C — Shirley Temple on the cover
A — Article on Shirley Temple
P — Picture or portrait
Numbers are the dates of publication

ABC Film Review (British): 4-54, 4-67
Ace Comics: 6-39
Action: 8-39 (C)
Advertising Age: 3-22-65
After Dark: 1970
Afternoon TV: 8-70
Alle Kvinneis (Norway) 3-7-39 (C & A)
America: 2-35, 9-16-67
American: 8-34 (P), 2-35 (A), 4-37, 5-37, 7-37, 11-37, 10-39, 11-39, 7-44
American Education: 12-70 (P)
American Collector: 7-75 (A)
American Girl 3-38, 8-41 (A), 1-71
American Home: 4-45 (A), 12-58 (A), 5-61 (A)
American Mercury: 8-34, 2-35
American Women
Andre de Dievers (French) (P)
Antique Journal 11-66
Antique News: 5-15-71
Antique Trader: 11-9-71, 8-15-72, 4-24-73, 9-25-73, 11-13-73, 5-14-74 (A) 7-2-74, 6-10-75, 4-22-75 (A), 7-8-75
Antiquiting: 7-1-73
Aunt Jane's Sewing Circle: 7-74
Australian Women's Weekly: 1-1-58 (P) 9-25-74
Australian Photoplay:
Better Home & Gardens: 9-38 (A), 3-50, 2-63, 12-73
Billboard: 6-23-34, 8-25-34, 11-10-34, 12-25-34, 5-25-35, 4-13-35, 11-30-35, 10-17-35, 12-28-35, 12-12-36, 12-13-41, 2-14-42
Book Review Digest: 1945
Box Office: 5-5-45
Boy's Life: 5-38
British Photoplay: 5-58 (A)
Calling All Girls: 10-41 (C), 2-42, 4-44 (C), 11-58 (A)
Canada Calls You: 1939 (P)
Canadian Home Journal: 3045
Capper's Farmer: 12-35, 1-37, 1-36, 11-47, 11-49
Carnation, The: 3-37 (A)
Carole Lombard's Life Story: 1942
Cavalier: 7-67
Ceramic Teacher: 1976
Chicago Summer: 1967
Child Life: 1-35, 4-35, 5-35, 9-35, 3-36, 7-36, 8-36, 10-36, 11-36, 12-36, 1-37, 5-37, 6-37, 9-37, 10-37, 11-37, 12-37, 7-38, 9-38, 2-40, 6-40
Cinema, The (British): 7-29-36, 1-4-39, 5-26-48, 6-11-48
Cinema (Italian): 1935, 3-10-37, 11-25-37, 10-17-37, 1938 (P), 2-38
Cinema Arts: 6-37, 9-37
Cinegraf (French): 1934, 1935 (C), 1936 (C), 1937
Cinema Reporter: 2-17-45 (C)

Cinemonde: 1966 (?) Color cover & article
Classic Film Collector: Fall 1973
Cinema Scene: 10-72
Cinema Reporter: 2-17-45 (C)
Cine-Revelation (French): 1954 (A), 1-5-36
Cine-Revue (Belgium): 9-23-49 (C), 7-27-71 (P&A)
Cine-Post: 11-27-35
Cine-Vogue: 12-19-47
Cine-Vue: 7-15-47 (A)
Clear Creek: 10-72
Click: 6-38, 12-38 (C), 11-40
Collector, The: 6-75
Collector's Journal (British): Winter 1965 (A)
Colliers: 10-12-35, 12-28-35 (P), 9-19-36 (P), 7-23-38, 3-25-38, 3-25-39, 5-31-47, 1-25-47, 8-2-47, 12-17-49, 10-11-52 (A)
Collectors Den
Coast: 12-75
Comfort: 12-36
Complete TV: 1-58 (P)
Commonwealth: 8-17-34 (A), 7-24-36, 11-5-37, 3-25-38, 7-7-39
Collector's News: 6-71, 10-73, 3-74 (A), 6-75, 5-75
Collector's Weekly: 3-23-71 (P&A)
Coronet: 7-47, 3-58 (A), 3-61 (A), 3-68, 12-72, 2-73 (C), 11-73, 10-74
Cosmopolitan: 4-37, 7-37, 10-37, 12-37, 3-39, 3-45, 4-47, 4-48, 1-49 (A), 2-51
Country Gentleman: 2-35 (A), 8-35, 11-36, 12-36, 1-37, 5-37, 7-37, 8-37, 10-37, 11-37, 12-37, 1-38, 6-38, 12-38
Cue: 12-6-41 (C)
Cracked: 1-72
Current Biographies: 10-45 (A)
Current Events: 7-31-36 (C)
Daily Film Renter (British): 7-2-42, 4-9-45 (P), 2-12-45, 6-27-45, 8-2-45, 10-22-45
Dell Comics: 1949
Delineator: 1-35, 3-37
Der Nene Film Kalendar (German) 1950
Dig: 8-61
Disney News: Summer 1973
Dog Craft: 12-38 (C)
Doll Talk: 7-8-63
Domenica del Corriere (Spain) 3-75 (A)
Dynamite: 4-74
Earnshaws Review: 8-67
Eastern Antiquity: 12-70
Ebony: 3-76 (A)
Eiga No Tomo: 5-50 (C)
The Elks: 8-34 (P), 7-38
Esquire: 1963, 6-66, 10-67, 1-68, 12-72 (A), 1-70

Etude: 3-40
TX Exhibitor, The: 5-27-42, 5-7-47
Express Messenger: 1935 (C)
Family Circle: 6-29-34, 8-10-34 (C), 12-7-34, 1-18-35, 5-17-35 (C), 7-12-35 (C), 9-13-35 (C), 1-24-36 (C), 6-26-36 (C), 7-24-36 (P), 10-16-36, 11-20-36, 1-29-37, 8-13-37 (C), 11-19-37 (C), 4-15-38 (C), 6-10-38 (C), 6-17-38 (A), 8-5-38, 12-9-38, 5-12-39 (C), 6-2-39, 7-21-39, 3-24-39 (C), 3-1-40, 12-12-41, 5-29-42 (C), 9-8-44 (C), 1-19-45 (C), 10-19-45, 12-57 (A), 6-61 (P), 1-69
Family Health: 9-72, 1-73 (A)
Farmer's Wife: 12-36, 3-37
Farm Journal: 11-36, 12-36, 12-37, 4-38, 8-38, 10-38, 1-39, 8-47
Festival (Belgium): 2-28-51 (C), 1950 (C)
Film Daily: 20th Anniv. 1938
Film Fun: 1932, 4-33
Film International: 7-75
Film Journal Advertiser: 4-70
Filmland: 11-49, 1-50 (C&A), 1-55
Film Pictorial (British): 4-20-34, 7-14-34 (A), 7-22-34 (C), 12-29-34 (C), 3-8-35 (C), 4-20-35, 3-16-35 (A), 5-4-35 (P), 3-23-35, 9-7-35 (C), 9-21-35 (A), 12-28-35 (A), 1-25-36, 2-22-36, 4-11-36, 4-25-36 (C&A), 8-1-36 (C&A), 8-8-36 (A), 9-25-36, 10-17-36 (A), 12-5-36 (P), 12-12-36, 12-26-36, 1-2-37 (P), Annual 1937 (A&P), Summer Special 1937 (P), 4-17-37 (P), 6-12-37, 7-17-37, 7-31-37 (C&A), 12-25-37, 1-15-38, 1-29-38, 2-5-38, 4-16-38, 7-30-38, Summer Extra 1938 (P), 8-27-38, 10-9-38 (P), 10-29-38, 11-26-38, 12-10-38 (P), 2-18-39, 3-4-39 (P), 4-8-39, 4-29-39, 5-8-39, 3-4-39 (P), 4-29-39, 5-8-39, 6-24-39, 7-15-39, 5-27-39, 8-5-39 (C&A)
Films & Filming: 12-67, 1-74 (P)
Films In Review: 2-61, 3-61, 4-62, 5-63
Film Weekly (British): 4-20-34, 8-3-34, 11-20-34, 10-18-34, 3-22-35, 4-26-35 (A), 5-31-35, 8-23-35 (C), 10-11-35 (A), 10-18-35, 12-28-35, 4-4-36 (A),6-27-36 (A), 7-11-36, 8-1-36, 10-3-36, 10-17-36 (P), 11-7-36 (A), 11-21-36, 12-5-36, 12-19-36, 12-26-36 (A), 3-27-37, 4-17-37, 6-26-37 (C), 9-37 (A), 10-23-37, 1-12-38, 1-15-38, 1-22-38, 3-19-38, 4-16-38, 5-14-38, 5-21-38, 5-28-38, 7-2-38, 7-18-38, 9-10-38 (P), 11-12-38, 12-24-38, 4-1-39, Summer Extra 1939 (P), 8-12-39 (C), 10-19-40
Fleetway: 1961 (A)
Flower Grower: 9-40, 12-38
Focus: 5-19-38
Focus On Films: Summer 1974

Mon Film (French): 4-6-49

Moose: 12-38 (P)

Motion Picture: 11-32, 12-32, 8-34, 9-34, 10-34 (C&A), 11-34, 1-35 (P), 2-35 (P), 3-35, 4-35 (P), 6-35 (A), 7-35, 8-35, 9-35 (A), 11-35, 1-36 (A), 2-36, 3-36 (C&A), 4-36, 5-36, 7-36 (A), 9-36, 10-36, 11-36, 1-37 (A), 2-37, 3-37, 6-37, 7-37 (A), 8-37, 10-37, 11-37 (P), 2-38 (A), 4-38, 5-38, 8-38, 9-38, 10-38 (P), 1-39 (P), 4-39, 7-39 (A), 9-40 (A), 10-40, 8-41, 1-42 (P), 6-42 (C), 8-42 (A), 9-43, 2-44 (A), 6-44, 7-44, 8-44, 11-44, 1-45 (A), 7-45 (A), 12-45 (A), 1-46, 2-46, 3-46 (C&A), 8-46 (A), 11-46, 1-47, 6-47, 7-47, 8-47, 11-47 (A), 5-48, 8-48 (C&A), 11-48 (A), 2-49 (C&A), 7-49 (C&A), 10-49, 12-49 (A), 1-50, 2-50, 4-50, 7-50, 8-50 (A), 11-50 (C&A), 12-50, 4-52, 8-52, 3-51 (A), 7-51, 8-53, 7-54 (A), 5-58, 9-67, 12-69, 9-70, 3-71 (A), 5-71, 7-71, 11-72, 2-73, 4-73 (A), 5-75

Motion Picture Herald: 11-3-33, 5-12-34, 5-19-34 (P), 6-9-34, 6-30-34 (P), 7-14-34 (P), 10-27-34, 12-1-34 (P), 12-15-34, 12-22-34, 12-29-34, 1-19-35, 2-2-35, 5-18-35 (P), 5-4-35 (P), 6-1-35 (P), 8-10-35 (P), 8-24-35, 12-28-35, 2-8-36, 6-11-35, 3-21-36, 4-11-36 (P), 4-4-36, 7-4-36, 7-3-37, 7-10-37, 10-9-37 (P), 10-16-37, 7-23-38, 6-10-39 (P), 6-24-39, 8-25-45, 10-6-45, 1-26-46, 2-2-46, 11-5-49 (P)

Motion Picture Star Album: 1948 (P&A)

Movie Album: 1941 (P)

Movie Classic: 12-1932, 5-34, 6-34 (P), 7-34, 9-34 (P), 10-34 (A), 11-34, 12-34 (A), 2-35 (A), 3-35 (A), 4-35, 5-35 (P), 6-35, 7-35 (A), 9-35 (P), 10-35 (A), 12-35 (A), 1-36, 2-36 (C&A), 3-36 (A), 4-36 (A), 5-36 (A), 6-36 (A), 7-36 (A), 9-36, 1-37 (P)

Movie Classics: 6-73, 10-73

Movie Digest: 5-72, 9-72, 3-73

Movie Fan Album: Winter 1946 (P), Winter 1947, 3-48 (P), Summer 1948, May-June 1949, Jan-Feb 1950, Mar-Apr. 1950 (P), May-June 1950

Movie Glamour: Vol. 1 No. 1

Moviegoer: 11-20-36

Movie Humor: 11-34

Movie Greats: 1971 (C&P)

Movieland: 9-43, 5-44, 6-44 (A), 10-44, 1-45 (C&A), 4-45, 7-45, 12-45, 4-46, 5-46 (A), 10-46, 3-47, 4-47 (A), 6-47 (C), 7-47 (P), 8-47, 11-47, 7-48, 8-48 (A), 11-48, 2-49 (A), 4-49, 6-49, 7-49, 10-49 (C&A), 12-49 (A), 1-50 (A), 4-53 (A), 7-58, 3-64

Movieland and TV Time: 2-67, 1-70, 6-70, 3-73

Movie Life: 11-37 (P), 12-37, 1-38 (P), 2-38 (P), 4-38, 6-38 (C), 7-38 (P), 9-38 (A), 11-38, 2-39 (C&P), 11-39, 12-39 (C), 1-40, 3-40, 10-40 (P), 3-41, 6-41 (P), 7-41 (P), 1-42 (A), 2-42, 6-42 (A), 12-42, 4-43, 8-43 (A), 12-43,

4-44 (A), 6-44, 8-44 (A), 12-44 (P), 4-45 (A), 6-45 (P&A), 7-45, 8-45 (C), 9-45, 11-45, 12-45 (P), Yearbook 1946, 2-46, 4-46, 5-46, 6-46, 10-46 (P), 11-46 (P), 12-46 (P), 2-47 (A), 4-47, 6-47 (C), 8-47, 11-47 (A), 1947 Yearbook, 2-48 (C&A), Yearbook 1948 (P), 5-48 (C), 9-48 (P), Yearbook 1949 (A), 1-49, 2-49 (A), 3-49 (A), 5-49 (C&A), 7-49, 9-49, 10-49 (P), 11-49 (A), 12-49, 1-50 (C), 2-50 (P), 5-50, 7-50 (A), 12-50 (P&A), 3-51, 4-51 (P), 2-53, 8-53, Yearbook 1954, 5-58, 10-58, 12-60, 2-68

Movie News: 8-23-35

Movie Mirror: 11-33, 2-34, 7-34 (A), 8-34 (A), 9-34 (P), 10-34 (A), 12-34 (C&P), 1-35 (A), 2-35 (A), 3-35, 4-35 (P), 5-35, 6-35 (P), 7-35 (A), 9-35, 10-35 (C), 12-35 (A), 1-36 (P), 2-36, 3-36 (P), 5-36 (C&A), 7-36 (P), 8-36 (A), 11-36, 12-36 (A), 1-37 (P), 2-37 (C), 3-37, 4-37, 5-37 (P), 6-37, 7-37 (P), 8-37 (A), 9-37, 10-37 (A), 11-37 (P), 12-37 (A), 1-38, 2-38 (C), 3-38, 4-38 (P), 5-38 (C), 8-38 (P), 9-38 (A), 10-38, 3-39 (A), 4-39, 5-39, 6-39 (A), 8-39 (P), 10-39 (A), 11-39, 12-39, 3-30, 4-30, 5-40 (C&A), 6-40, 10-40

Movie Pix: 2-36 (A), 3-38 (P), 10-49 (A), 7-49 (A)

Movie Play: 4-36 (A), Winter 1944, 9-44 (A), 11-49, 3-54

Movie Radio Guide: 2-17-40 (A), 3-24-40 (A), 3-16-40 (A), 3-23-40 (C), 5-18-40 (P&A), 7-20-40, 8-10-40, 7-7-40 (P), 7-21-40 (C&A), 7-28-40, 10-5-40, 11-9-40, 3-1-41, 3-8-41, 9-20-41 (A), 10-6-41, 12-6-41 (C&A), 11-29-41, 5-9-42 (A), 5-23-42 (P), 9-43 (A)

Movies: 10-33, 8-34 (C&A), 9-35 (P), 3-38, 11-39 (P), 2-40 (A), 4-40, 9-40, 6-42 (P), 7-42 (P), 11-43, 1-44, 5-44 (P), 10-44, 12-44, 2-45, 3-45 (A), 5-45 (C), 5-46, 2-47, 3-47, 4-47 (P), 8-47, 9-47 (A), 10-47 (C), 11-47, 10-53

Movie Screen: 1938

Movie Show: 11-44, 12-45, 1-46 (P), 8-46 (P), 3-47 (A), 4-47 (P), 7-47, 8-47 (P), 12-47 (A)

Movie Songs: 7-46

Movie Stars: 4-61 (A), 7-61, 4-62, 8-63, 8-64, 8-70, 4-72, 9-72 (A), 12-72 (A)

Movie Stars Parade: 2-41 (P), 8-41 (P), 1-42 (A), 11-43, 8-42 (C&P&A), 12-42 (A), 12-43, 4-44 (C&A), 10-44, 4-45 (P), 9-45 (P), 10-45 (C), 12-45 (A), 5-46 (A), 7-46 (A), 9-46 (P), 12-46 (C&A), 4-47, 1-47, 10-47 (A), 1-48 (C), 7-48, 8-48 (C&A), 11-48 (A), 1-49, 2-49 (C), 5-49, 7-49, 11-49 (C&A), 1-50 (A), 2-50, 3-50, 8-50 (A), 5-51 (A), 7-56

Movie Story: 1-36 (A), 5-37, 7-37 (A), 3-38 (A), 10-38, 12-38 (A), 1-39, 4-39 (A(, 6-39, 8-39 (C&A), 12-39, 2-40 (A), 8-40 (A), 6-42 (A), 4-44, 3-46, 10-46, 1-47, 3-47 (A), 7-47, 8-47,

Yearbook 1947 (P&A), Yearbook 1948 (A), 5-48 (A), 3-49 (C&A), 5-49 (A), 4-50

Movie TV & Photo Stars: 9-71 (A)

Movie World: 12-69

My Weekly Reader: 4-3-39, 9-11-39 (A)

Nation: 9-18-67, 10-30-67, 12-4-67

National Enquirer: 1-11-70 (A), 7-26-70, 5-17-70 (C&A), 10-3-71 (P&A), 4-15-75 (A), 4-76 (A&P), 6-22-76 (A&P)

National Geographic: 9-38, 8-63

National Observer: 5-5-73 (A&P)

National Legionaire: 7-38

National Star Chronicle: 1963

National Tattler: 10-11-70, 12-10-72 (A)

National Wildlife: 6-73, 7-73, 12-73, 1-74 (A)

New Republic: 11-25-67, 5-16-34

New England Grocery & Market Mag: 7-37 (P)

Nevada Highways & Parks: Spring 1968

Newsday: 6-24-69 (A), 6-13-68 (A)

News Review (British): 12-17-36

Newsweek: 4-15-33, 5-26-34, 7-28-34 (A), 5-16-36, 6-27-36, 7-24-37, 1-2-39, 3-20-39 (P), 6-26-39, 1-1-40, 2-5-40, 5-20-40, 12-15-41, 5-25-42, 7-10-44, 7-24-44, 9-18-44, 10-1-45, 10-3-49 (A), 2-13-50, 4-29-57, 9-29-58, 12-21-60, 4-29-63, 12-7-64, 6-28-65, 12-13-65, 6-12-67, 6-19-67, 9-11-67, 10-30-67, 11-6-67, 7-15-68, 9-2-68, 11-27-67, 9-29-69, 11-20-72, 6-16-75 (A), 2-9-76

Nord France: 10-2-48, 5-14-49

Nostalgia Illustrated: 12-74 (C&A)

Novella: 8-9-58 (A)

New Movie Mag: 5-34 (P), 7-34, 8-34 (P), 9-34, 10-34 (A), 11-34, 12-34, 2-35, 4-35 (A&P), 8-35 (P)

Oggi (Italian): 11-23-72 (P), 1975 (P&A)

Old Hollywood: 1956 (P)

On The Q.T.: 10-55

Opera News: 1972

Our Dumb Animals: 2-40 (A&P)

Pageant: 11-49, 4-68, 1-69, 7-71 (A)

Pagina: 1950's

Palm Springs: 1935-36 (P)

Parents: 11-34, 1-35, 2-35, 4-35, 9-35, 4-36 (P), 8-36, 9-36, 2-37 (P), 10-37, 8-38, 10-38 (C&A), 8-39 (C), 4-39, 10-41 (P), 10-47, 4-48, 12-49, 8-58 (C&P), 5-61

Pathfinder: 10-24-36, 8-13-38, 9-3-38, 11-28-38, 10-1-45, 5-21-47, 10-8-47, 12-17-47, 6-16-48

People: 9-9-74 (P), 5-12-75

Photoplay: 11-32, 12-32 (P), 1-33, 7-33 (P), 11-33, 1-34, 4-34, 6-34, 7-34, 8-34 (A), 9-34, 10-34, 11-34 (A), 12-34 (P), 1-35 (C), 2-35 (P), 3-35, 4-35, 5-35 (P), 6-35, 7-35 (P), 8-35, 9-35, 10-35 (P), 12-35 (A), 1-36, 2-36 (P), 3-36 (C), 4-36 (A), 5-36, 6-36 (P), 7-36, 8-36 (A), 10-36, 11-36, 12-36 (C), 1-37 (A), 3-37 (A), 4-37, 5-37 (P), 6-37 (A), 7-37, 8-37, 9-37 (A), 10-37,

Screen Legends: 8-65
Screen Life: 3-40, 9-41
Screen Lovers: 1955
Screen News (British): 3-26-38
Screen Pictorial (British): 5-36 (P),
 11-36, Winter Annual 1937 (P)
Screen Play: 1-33, 4-34, 5-34, 7-34 (P),
 8-34, 9-34 (A), 10-34 (C), 2-35, 5-35
 (A), 7-35 (A), 12-35 (P), 1-36 (C&A),
 3-36, 4-36, 5-36 (C&A), 6-36 (A),
 9-36, 10-36, 11-36, 1-37, 3-37 (C), 6-37,
 8-37 (C&A), 12-37 (P)
Screen Romances: 4-34 (P), 7-34, 8-34
 (A), 11-34, 2-35 (A), 4-35, 6-35 (A),
 12-35 (P), 3-36 (A), 4-36, 5-36 (P),
 7-36 (A), 10-36 (A&C) 2-37 (A), 5-37
 (P), 6-37 (P), 7-37 (A), 9-37, 11-37
 (C&A), 2-38 (P), 5-38, 7-38 (A),
 11-38, 12-38 (A), 1-39, 4-39 (A), 8-39
 (A), 8-40 (C&A), 3-40, 5-41, 8-41,
 2-42, 1-44, 8-44, 12-44 (P), 5-45 (P&A),
 9-45, 10-45 (C&A), 9-46, 12-46, 3-47
 (C&A), 4-47, 6-47, 12-47 (A), 4-48
Screen Secrets (British): 1948 (A)
Screen Stars: 6-44 (A), 7-45, 9-45 (P),
 10-45, 4-46, 9-46 (A), 5-47, 10-47,
 10-49, 2-50 (A), 12-50 (C&A), 4-51,
 1-55
Screen Stories: 4-48, 5-48 (C&A), 8-48,
 9-48, 2-49, 3-49 (A), 4-49, 5-49 (A),
 11-49, 12-49 (A), 2-50 (A), 3-50,
 4-53, 3-58, 6-58 (A), 10-58 (A), 2-59,
 6-61, 6-62, 12-63, 2-64, 2-68, 6-69,
 9-71, 9-72(A), 3-73
Screen World: 4-50 (A)
See: 3-9-38 (A)
Senior Scholastic: 11-18-66
Serenade: 6-35
Seventeen: 9-44, 11-70, 10-71 (A), 1-73
Shadowplay: 6-34, 7-34, 10-34 (C), 2-35,
 5-35
Shirley Temple's 21st Birthday Album:
 1949
Show: 8-62 (P), July-Aug. 1967 (P),
 Mar.-Apr. 1967 (P)
Show Business Illustrated: 10-3-61
Show (Manila): 7-70, (P&A)
Showman's Trade Review: 12-22-45,
 1-5-46, 2-9-46 (P)
Silver Screen: 5-34, 8-34 (P), 9-34 (A),
 10-34, 11-34, 12-34 (P), 3-35 (C&A),
 4-35, 5-35, 6-35 (A), 7-35 (A), 9-35, 10-35,
 (A), 11-35, 12-35 (C&A), 1-36 (A),
 2-36, 3-36 (A), 4-36, 5-36, 6-36 (C&A),
 8-36, 9-36, 11-36, 12-36 (A), 1-37 (A),
 2-37, 4-37, 5-37, 9-37, 12-37, 2-38,
 3-38 (A), 4-38 (A), 5-38, 6-38 (P),
 8-38 (A), 9-38, 10-38 (P), 11-38 (C),
 11-38 (C), 1-39, 4-39 (P), 5-39 (C), 8-39
 (A), 9-39, 2-40, 3-40 (P), 4-40, 8-40,
 11-40, 5-41, 7-41, 11-41, 2-42, 6-42 (P),
 8-42, 4-43, 1-44 (C&P), 10-44 (P),
 12-44, 1-45 (P), 8-45 (A), 12-45 (A),
 3-46, 1-47 (A), 2-47, 5-47, 7-47, 3-48
 (P), 8-48, 2-49 (A), 3-49 (C), 5-49, 6-49,
 10-49 (A), 12-49, 1-50 (A), 8-53 (A),
 2-68 (A), 5-72, 2-73
Simplicity Sewing Book: Spring 1960
Sir: 2-45 (A), 1-51

Song Hit Folio: 1934 (P)
Song Hits: 9-35 (C), 8-37 (C&A)
Song Review: 4-38, 6-38, 9-38, 10-38,
 12-38, 1-39, 1-40, 4-40, 10-40
Stage: 6-35, 7-38
Stand-By: 10-10-36
Stardom: 6-42, 1-44 (A)
St. Nicholas Mag: 1-37 (A), 8-37 (A),
 3-38 (A), 7-38 (A), 3-39 (A), 7-39 (A)
Successful Farming: 12-36, 3-37, 4-38,
 11-45, 7-49
Suppressed: (A)
Teen: 7-61, 7-67, 7-68
Teen World: 4-62
Tempo (Italy): 3-14-70 (A)
Theatre Arts Monthly: 6-35, 10-51
This Was Hollywood: 1955 (C)
This Was Show Business: 1956
Time: 4-30-34, 7-23-34, 10-10-34,
 12-31-34, 3-11-35, 6-17-35, 5-12-35,
 12-30-35, 4-27-36 (C&A), 7-6-36,
 8-10-36 (P), 10-19-36, 12-28-36, 5-3-37,
 7-19-37, 10-25-37, 1-3-38, 3-21-38,
 4-23-38, 7-4-38, 8-1-38, 9-5-38, 1-2-39,
 3-20-39, 5-1-39, 7-3-39, 7-17-39, 8-8-41,
 3-9-42, 5-1-44 (A), 1-8-45 (C), 6-25-45,
 8-13-45, 10-22-45, 2-2-48, 5-31-48,
 10-24-49, 1-27-58 (A), 9-8-67, 11-10-48,
 6-28-68, 9-2-68, 5-22-72, 6-26-72,
 9-4-72 (P), 11-4-74
Today's Health: 11-60 (A), 4-62
Today's Women: 6-49 (C&A)
Toy Pictorial: 1935
Tri State Trader: 11-22-68, 7-69,
 8-29-70 (A&P)
True Confessions: 7-35
True Experiences: 10-34 (P)
True Story: 4-36 (C&A), 8-38, 9-38
TV Album: 1958 (P)
TV Guide: 1-11-58 (A), 5-3-58 (C&A),
 6-14-58, 8-58, 11-28-59, 12-59 (A),
 12-3-60 (C&A), 7-11-64
TV Movie Screen: 1955 (P), 2-58, 9-58
 (A), 1959 (P), 1-61 (A), 6-62, 5-63 (A),
 6-65, 3-73 (C&A)
TV Movies Today: 10-70 (P), 12-74 (A)
TV News: 8-63
TV Picture Album: No. 11 (P)
TV Radio Album: 1958 (C&A), 1961
 (P&A)
TV Radio Annual: 1959 (P), 1961 (P)
TV Radio Life: 1-11-58 (C&A)
TV Radio Mirror: 1-58 (A), 10-60
 (C&A), 9-64, 12-64, 3-65, 9-65, 1-67,
 1-70, 2-71, 1-74
TV Star Annual: No. 4 1958 (A), No. 5
 1958 (C&A), No. 6 (P)
TV Star Parade: 1-58 (A), 2-58 (A),
 4-58 (P), 6-58, 7-58 (A), 12-60 (A),
 3-61
TV Week (Chicago Tribune): 11-23-57
 (A), 1-11-58 (C)
TV Yearbook: #9, #11
Uncensored: 8-56 (A), 11-58 (A)
U.S. Camera: 2-46, 9-46
U.S. News & World Report: 9-11-67 (A)
Vanity Fair: 9-34 (P), 11-34, 1-35, 4-35
 (P), 7-35, 9-35
Variety: 12-25-34, 1-1-36 (P), 7-20-66

Viva (Netherlands): 1976 (A)
Weekend (British): 7-7-65, 5-26-71
 (P&A)
Weekend (Netherlands): 6-21-75 (A)
Weekly Book Review: 11-18-45
Weiss Ruffili: 1943 (A)
West Coast Pedler: 11-15-72 (P&A),
 10-75
West Coast Review of Books: 4-75
 (C&P)
Western Antique Mart: 11-12-70
Who's Who In Hollywood: 1948, 1950
 (P), 1952, 1954, 1959 (P), 1962 (P),
 1963, 1965
Who's Who in TV and Radio: 1958
 (C&P), 1959, 1960, 1961
Woman: 12-25-65 (A)
Woman's Comfort: 9-68
Woman's Day: 6-38 (P), 8-38, 9-38 (A),
 12-38 (P), 8-42 (P), 9-44, 9-45, 9-48,
 9-67, 12-73, 4-76
Woman's Home Companion: 3-36 (P),
 8-36 (P), 6-37, 7-37, 11-37, 12-37,
 4-38, 6-38, 8-38, 11-38 (A), 6-39, 2-40,
 8-42 (P), 4-44 (P), 12-44 (A), 11-45,
 9-46, 10-46, 11-46, 12-46, 6-47, 9-47,
 2-48 (A), 6-49, 11-49 (P)
Women's Household: 3-71, 5-73
Woman's Own (British): 4-14-73 (A)
Woman's Pictorial (British): 3-20-37
Woman's World: 2-36, 9-36, 12-36, 2-37,
 7-37, 5-38, 8-38, 1-40, 5-76
Woman's Circle: 3-68, 7-69, 9-73
Wonderful World of Women: 1966
World: 11-7-72
Young America: 3-17-37, 2-2-40 (P)
Young Dancer: 11-36 (A)
Your Future For 1938 (P&A)

The following are newspaper items
concerning Shirley Temple.
9-3-32: Midweek Pictorial (P&A)
1934: Every Week (P&A)
6-17-34: Screen & Radio Weekly (P)
7-15-34: Screen & Radio Weekly
 (Cartoon)
9-9-34: Chicago Tribune (Full page
 color pic. & 2 pages pic)
9-9-34: Screen & Radio Weekly (Color
 pic)
12-16-34: Grit (A&P)
12-23-34: Denver Post Sunday Mag.
 (C&A)
1-6-35: The Times Picayune (New
 Orleans) (A&P)
2-3-35: Screen & Radio Weekly (Large
 color pic.)
4-19-35: North Adam's Transcript
 (Boston) (A&P)
4-14-35: Screen & Radio Weekly
 (Color cover & pic.)
5-5-35: This Week (Color cover & A)
8-4-35: Des Moines Sunday Register
 (P)
8-4-35: Chicago Sunday Tribune (P)
8-4-35: Screen & Radio Weekly (Color
 pic &A)
8-4-35: Milwaukee Journal (P)
8-11-35: Screen & Radio Weekly
 (Color pic)

8-11-35: Des Moines Sunday Register (P)

8-18-35: Des Moines Sunday Register (P)

8-25-35: Des Moines Sunday Register (P)

9-1-35: Des Moines Sunday Register (P)

9-1-35: Chicago Sunday Tribune (Color pic)

9-1-35: The Times Picayune (New Orleans) (A&P)

9-16-35: Youngstown Telegram (Ohio) (P)

9-17-35: Youngstown Telegram (Ohio) (P)

9-19-35: Youngstown Telegram (Ohio) (P)

10-6-35: Post Standard (P)

10-13-35: Screen & Radio Weekly (C)

10-15-35: Cincinnati Post (P)

10-16-35: Cincinnati Post (P)

11-8-35: Four Leaf Clover (C)

11-17-35: New York Sunday News (C)

12-7-35: Chicago Daily News (P)

12-14-35: Chicago Daily News (P)

12-21-35: Chicago Daily News (P)

12-22-35: Des Moines Sunday Register (Color pic)

12-28-35: Chicago Daily News (P)

1936: Uncle Ray's Corner Column

1936: This Week (A&P)

1936: This Week (Color pic)

1-4-36: Chicago Daily News (P)

1-11-36: Chicago Daily News (P)

1-12-36: Screen & Radio Weekly (Color pic)

1-18-36: Chicago Daily News (P)

1-19-36: Milwaukee Journal (P)

1-19-36: Screen & Radio Weekly (P)

2-22-36: Cleveland Press (P&A)

2-23-36: Screen & Radio Weekly (Color pic)

2-29-36: Chicago Daily News (P)

3-7-36: Chicago Daily News (P)

3-14-36: Chicago Daily News (P)

3-21-36: Chicago Daily News (P)

3-29-36: Chicago Sunday Tribune (P)

4-5-36: Chicago Sunday Tribune (P)

4-5-36: Youngstown (Ohio) Vindicator (P)

4-18-36: This Week (Color pic. & A)

4-19-36: Des Moines Sunday Register (P)

4-23-36: Appleton Post (Crescent, Wisc.) (A&P)

4-23-36: Oakland Shopping News (Calif) (P)

5-10-36: Screen & Radio Weekly (Color pic)

6-13-36: Screen & Radio Weekly: (P)

6-21-36: Screen & Radio Weekly (Color pic)

6-28-36: Screen & Radio Weekly (Color pic)

7-5-36: Screen & Radio Weekly (Color pic)

7-5-36: Philadelphia Record (P)

7-12-36: Chicago Sunday Tribune (P)

7-19-36: Sacramento Union (Calif.) (Color ad)

8-22-36: Saturday Home Mag (Journal American) (A&P)

8-23-36: Screen & Radio Weekly (Color pic)

8-29-36: Saturday Home Mag (Journal American) (A&P)

8-30-35: Sunday Journal (Minn.) (A&P)

9-20-36: Chicago Sunday Tribune (P)

10-4-36: Philadelphia Inquirier (P)

11-1-36: Chicago Sunday Tribune (C)

11-18-36: Chicago American (A)

11-19-36: Peoria Star

11-20-36: Chicago Tribune

11-23-36: Peoria Star

11-29-36: Peoria Star (Ill)

12-12-36: Omaha Bee News (Neb.)

12-13-36: New York Sunday Mirror

12-19-36: Peoria Star

12-20-36: Philadelphia Inquirer (C)

12-20-36: New York Sunday Mirror (C)

12-26-36: New York Journal American (P)

1-2-37: New York Journal American (A & color pic)

1-2-37: Chicago Daily News (A&P)

2-3-37: Chicago Tribune (A&P)

2-28-37: Screen & Radio Weekly (Color pic)

3-37: Washington (P)

3-7-37: Screen & Radio Weekly (Color pic)

3-25-37: Youngstown Vindicator (Ohio) (P&A)

3-27-37: Harrisburg Evening News (Pa.) (P)

4-16-37: Oakland Tribune (Calif.)

4-18-37: Times Picayune (A& color pic)

4-24-37: Chicago Daily News: (A&P)

4-25-37: New York Sunday Mirror (P)

4-25-37: New York Sunday Mirror (Color pic)

4-28-37: Chicago Daily News (P)

5-14-37: Boston Globe (P&A)

5-23-37: Times Picayune

6-13-37: New York Sunday Mirror

6-19-37: San Francisco Call Bulletin (Calif.) (P)

7-4-37: Chicago Tribune (P)

7-11-37: Times Picayune

7-17-37: New York Journal American (P)

7-18-37: Chicago Tribune (A&P)

1937: American Weekly

9-12-37: New York Sunday Mirror

9-12-37: Times Picayune

9-26-37: St. Louis Dispatch (A&P)

10-12-37: Milwaukee News (P)

10-24-37: Chicago Sunday Tribune (C)

10-27-37: Central, Ill. (A&P)

11-20-37: San Francisco Call Bulletin (Calif) (P)

12-2-37: Gem Theatre News (P&A)

12-5-37: Times Picayune (P&A)

12-17-37: New York Sunday Mirror (C)

12-21-37: New York Journal American (P)

12-26-37: Times Picayune (A&P)

12-19-37: Screen & Radio Weekly (C)

2-14-38: Tacoma (Wash) (P)

2-20-38: Chicago Tribune (Color Pic & A)

3-6-38: Chicago Sunday Tribune

3-6-38: Youngstown Vindicator (Ohio) (P)

4-3-38: New York Herald Tribune (P)

4-3-38: Philadelphia Inquirer (A&P)

4-17-38: New York Sunday Mirror (Color pic. & A)

4-17-38: Oakland Tribune (Calif) (Color pic & A)

4-17-38: Philadelphia Inquirer (C)

4-23-38: Chicago Daily News (A&P)

6-12-38: Screen & Radio Weekly (P&A)

6-12-38: New York Sunday News (C)

6-17-38: Chicago Times (P)

7-24-38: Screen & Radio Weekly (C)

7-31-38: Screen & Radio Weekly (C)

8-6-38: Kansas City Times (A&P)

9-18-38: Screen & Radio Weekly

9-22-38: Chicago Herald & Examiner (P)

10-16-38: Chicago Sunday Tribune (A&P)

11-20-38: Chicago & New York Journal American (Color pic.)

12-11-38: Los Angeles Times (Color pic)

12-25-38: Chicago Sunday Tribune (P)

1-1-39: Chicago Times (P)

1-15-39: Chicago Sunday Tribune (P)

1-22-39: Youngstown Vindicator (Ohio) (A&P)

2-19-39: Screen & Radio Weekly (C)

2-20-39: Chicago Tribune

March 1939: Baltimore American (P)

3-12-39: New York Sunday Mirror (Color pic)

3-26-39: Screen & Radio Weekly (A)

April 1939: Baltimore American (P)

4-23-39: Washington Sunday Star (D.C.) (A&P)

4-23-39: Screen & Radio Weekly (Color pic.)

5-7-39: Chicago Sunday Tribune (Color pic & A)

5-16-39: London Daily Sketch (England) (P)

6-3-39: Rhode Island Star Sun (A&P)

6-25-39: New York Journal American (P)

6-25-39: Chicago Herald & Examiner (P)

9-24-39: Chicago Herald & Examiner (A&P)

11-19-39: Philadelphia Inquirer (Color Pic)

12-17-39: Chicago Sunday Tribune (A&P)

12-24-39: Times Picayune (Color pic)

12-24-39: Screen & Radio Weekly (C)

12-24-39: Philadelphia Inquirer (P)

12-30-39: Philadelphia Inquirer (P&A)

1-21-40: Los Angeles Times (C)

1-26-40: Joliet Herald News (A&P)

2-11-40: Chicago Herald Examiner (P)

2-18-40: New York Journal American
(Color pic)

3-3-40: Screen & Radio Weekly:
(Color pic & A)

4-6-40: San Francisco Call Bulletin
(P&A)

4-28-40: Baltimore American (P&A)

5-5-40: Baltimore American (P&A)

5-12-40: Chicago Tribune (P)

6-7-40: Friday (C&A&P)

8-18-40: Chicago Herald American
(Color pic)

8-24-40: This Week (P&A)

9-1-40: New York Sunday Mirror
(P&A)

10-5-41: New York Sunday Mirror (P)

10-19-41: Chicago Sunday Tribune (P)

11-2-41: New York Times (C&P)

12-41: Milwaukee Journal (C)

12-17-41: New York Sunday News (C)

12-28-41: This Week (C&A)

1-25-42: Chicago Herald Tribune
(C & color pic)

1-25-42: New York Journal American
(A&P)

3-22-42: Chicago Sunday Tribune
(A&P)

3-22-42: Chicago Sun Times (A&P)

5-17-42: New York News (P)

6-14-42: Chicago Sunday Tribune (P)

6-21-42: American Weekly (A&P)

11-15-42: Chicago Sunday Tribune (P)

8-1-43: Chicago Sunday Tribune (A&P)

10-3-43: New York Times Mag. (C&A)

1944: Parade (P&A)

1944: Detroit News (A&P)

5-7-44: Chicago Sunday Tribune (A&P)

6-24-44: San Francisco Call Bulletin
(Color pic)

7-23-44: Herald American Pictorial
Review (P)

8-27-44: Chicago Sunday Tribune (P)

10-1-44: Pictorial Review (P)

10-8-44: Philadelphia Inquirer (C)

10-15-44: New York Sunday News
Mag. (C)

10-29-44: Chicago Sunday Tribune
(A&P)

1-21-45: Joliet Herald News

2-4-45: American Weekly

2-11-45: New York Times Mag. (A&P)

4-22-45: New York Sunday News (C)

5-20-45: Pictorial Review (Color pic &
(A)

6-3-45: Chicago Sunday Tribune (C)

6-10-45: Parade (P)

9-20-45: Chicago Herald American (P)

10-7-45: Chicago Sunday Tribune (C)

11-11-45: Chicago Sunday Tribune (P)

12-2-45: Chicago Sunday Tribune

12-23-45: American Weekly (A&P)

4-13-46: Chicago Daily News (C)

4-14-46: American Weekly (A&P)

5-19-46: Pictorial Review (C)

12-15-46: St. Paul Sunday Pioneer
Press (A&P)

12-15-46: Chicago Sunday Tribune
(Color pic & A)

3-9-47: Chicago Sunday Tribune (A&P)

5-11-47: This Week

5-18-47: American Weekly

5-25-47: Parade

7-27-47: Pictorial Review (C)

8-3-47: Parage (P)

1-4-48: Chicago Sunday Tribune (C)

3-21-48: New York Sunday Mirror (C)

1948: Pictorial Review (P)

7-17-48: Chicago Daily News (C)

7-25-48: Chicago Sunday Tribune (C)

8-7-48: Los Angeles Examiner (Color
pic)

8-8-48: New York Sunday Mirror (C)

8-15-48: Chicago Sunday Tribune
(A&P)

12-5-48: New York Sunday News (P)

12-19-48: New York Sunday Mirror (C)

2-26-49: Los Angeles Examiner
(Color pic)

5-8-49: Chicago Sunday Tribune (C)

11-27-49: New York Sunday Mirror (C)

3-12-50: Grit (A&P)

7-2-50: American Weekly (C)

9-17-50: Chicago Herald American (P)

10-7-50: Los Angeles Examiner
(Color pic)

3-4-51: American Weekly (A&P)

3-11-51: American Weekly (A&P)

2-8-53: American Weekly (A&P)

9-11-55: Kansas City Star (A&P)

10-9-55: Chicago Sunday Tribune (P)

4-10-57: Minneapolis Star (A&P)

8-57: Dayton Journal (Ohio) (P)

9-1-57: Parade (P)

10-20-57: Parade (C&A&P)

11-15-57: Los Angeles Times

1-20-57: Chicago Sun Times

12-15-57: Milwaukee Journal (P&A)

1-12-58: New York Journal American
(C)

3-2-58: Miami News (A&P)

3-30-58: New York Sunday News
(C&A)

4-6-58: Miami News (P&A)

4-13-58: Chicago Tribune (A&P)

4-13-58: Chicago Sunday Tribune
(A&P)

5-9-58: Chicago Sun Times (P&A)

5-25-58: American Weekly (A&P)

7-27-58: Chicago Sun Times (A&P)

9-17-58: Chicago American (A&P)

9-24-58: Chicago Sun Times (A&P)

11-2-58: Parade (C&A)

11-16-58: Parade (P)

12-21-58: Milwaukee Journal (A)

11-26-59: Chicago Tribune

4-24-60: Chicago Tribune (A&P)

11-27-60: Chicago Tribune (A&P)

12-4-60: Chicago Sunday Tribune
(A&P)

12-25-60: Parade (A&P)

6-11-61: New York Sunday News
(Color pic)

6-10-62: This Week (C&A)

3-25-62: Chicago Tribune (A&P)

9-30-62: Shreveport Times Sunday
Mag. (La.) (Color pic. & A)

4-23-63: Los Angeles Herald
Examiner (A&P)

5-5-63: Grit

10-6-63: San Francisco Examiner
Weekly (A)

8-8-64: Anchorage Daily News (Alaska)
(A&P)

3-10-65: Daily Telegraph (British)
(A&P)

3-16-65: Daily Mirror (British)
(A&P)

4-65: Modern World (Australia) (A&P)

4-18-65: Wichita Eagle (Kansas)

6-19-65: Oakland Tribune (A&P)

7-7-65: Weekend Mag. (P)

2-20-66: San Francisco Examiner
(A&P)

2-24-66: New York Journal American
(A&P)

12-1-66: Waukesha Freeman (Wisc.)

12-27-66: Los Angeles Herald
Examiner (A&P)

9-3-67: San Francisco Examiner
(A&P)

9-10-67: Akron Beacon Journal (Ohio)
(A&P)

9-14-67: Redwood City Tribune
(Calif) (A&P)

9-24-67: Los Angeles Examiner (A&P)

9-27-67: Women's Wear Daily (A&P)

10-1-67: Detroit News (A&P)

10-10-67: Evening News & Chronicle
(British) (A&P)

10-19-67: Chicago Daily News (A&P)

10-22-67: Sunday Mail (British)
(A&P)

10-22-67: Chicago Sun Times (A&P)

10-24-67: London Daily Sketch
(British) (A&P)

11-5-67: Los Angeles Times West
Mag. (A&P)

11-12-67: Chicago Sunday Tribune
Mag. (A&P)

12-16-67: Honolulu Advertiser (A&P)

12-31-67: Parade (A&P)

2-20-68: Waukegan News-Sun (Ill.)
(A&P)

4-20-68: The Truth (Elkhart, Ind.)
(A&P)

4-21-68: San Francisco Examiner
(A&P)

4-23-68: Milwaukee Sentinel (A&P)

5-9-68: Honolulu Star Bulletin (A&P)

6-2-68: Milwaukee Journal

6-20-68: Fairbanks Daily News
(Alaska) (A&P)

6-21-68: Anchorage Daily News
(Alaska) (A&P)

6-28-68: Times-Fairbanks, Alaska
(A&P)

9-30-68: Manchester Evening (British)
(A&P)

10-22-68: Daily Olympian (Wash)
(A&P)

7-6-69: Milwaukee Journal

8-13-69: Puyallup Valley Tribune
(Wash)

12-11-69: Salinas Journal (Kansas)
(A&P)

12-12-69: New York Times (A&P)

12-15-69: Evening Standard (British)
(A&P)

12-23-69: Chicago Today (A&P)
12-9-69: Oakland Tribune (A&P)
2-1-70: Chicago Tribune (A&P)
1-70: New York Sunday News (A&P)
1-10-70: San Francisco Examiner
(A&P)
3-22-70: Joliet Herald News (A&P)
3-22-70: Los Angeles Times (A&P)
4-2-70: Los Angeles Herald Examiner
(A&P)
4-5-70: Chicago Sun Times (A&P)
4-26-70: Los Angeles Times West
Mag. (Color pic)
5-9-70: Aurora Beacon News (Ill.)
P&A)
9-3-70: Wichita Eagle (Kansas)
9-70: Victorville (Calif) (A&P)
10-11-70: Grit (Color pic & A)
11-22-70: Sunday Denver Post (A&P)
12-6-70: St. Louis Post Dispatch (A&P)
1-17-71: Sunday Post Tribune
3-8-71: Palo Alto Times (Calif) (A&P)
6-13-71: Joliet Herald News
3-13-72: Washington Evening Star
(D.C.) (A&P)
3-19-72: Grit (A&P)
3-26-72: Family Weekly (A&P)
7-7-72: Beverly Hills Courier (Calif)
(A&P)
7-20-72: Napperville Sun (Ill)
10-13-72: Palm Beach Times (Calif)
(A&P)
11-72: Chicago Tribune Mag. (A&P)
11-12-72: Milwaukee Journal (A&P)
11-12-72: Detroit Free Press (A&P)
11-12-72: San Jose Mercury & News
(Calif) (A)
11-19-72: Indianapolis Star Mag.
(A&P)
8-8-72: Chicago Today (A&P)
12-22-72: The Blade (Toledo, Ohio)
12-31-72: Chicago Today (A&P)
1-12-73: Tehonsha Idea (Mich)
1-10-73: Utrechts Nieuwshlad
(Netherlands) (A&P)
2-26-73: Chicago Tribune (A&P)
4-1-73: Shreveport Times (La) (A&P)
4-4-73: Community Advisor
(Marshall, Mich.)
5-6-73: Chicago Sunday Tribune (A&P)
5-24-73: New York Daily News
7-15-73: Sunday Bulletin (Pa.) (A&P)
7-29-73: Fresno Bee (Calif) (A&P)
8-3-73: Chicago Today
8-16-73: Chicago Tribune (A&P)
8-23-73: Hutchinson News (Kansas)
(Color pic & A)
9-3-73: Los Angeles Herald Examiner
(P&A)
9-9-73: New York Times Mag.
11-23-73: Detroit Free Press (A&P)
12-31-73: Los Angeles Times (P&A)
4-28-74: Fresno Bee (Calif) (A&P)
5-14-74: Daily Pilot (Costa Mesa,
Calif.)
6-22-74: Chicago Daily News (A&P)
8-28-74: Fresno Bee (A&P)
9-8-74: Chicago Tribune (A&P)
9-9-74: People (A&P)

9-11-74: Chicago Sun Times (A&P)
9-25-74: Australian Women's Weekly
10-4-74: Chicago Daily News (A&P)
11-10-74: Family Weekly-Joliet
Herald News (C&A)
11-20-74: The World (Naperville, Ill)
(A&P)
12-11-74: San Antonio Express (A&P)
12-29-74: Amarillo Globe Times (Tex)
3-14-75: Chicago Daily News (A&P)
3-30-75: The Courier Journal &
Times (Kentucky) (A&P)
4-10-75: Daily Mirror (British) (A&P)
5-11-75: Sunday Times Mag (British)
(A&P)
7-27-75: Sunday Herald Advertiser
(Boston) (C&A)
10-10-75: San Francisco Chronicle
(A&P)
10-26-75: Chicago Sunday Tribune (P)
11-23-75: Chicago Sunday Tribune
(A&P)
11-30-75: Bloomfield (Colo.)
1-23-76: San Francisco Chronicle
(A&P)
1-25-76: Chicago Sunday Tribune
(A&P)
4-29-76: Washington Post (D.C.) (A&P)
6-13-76: Chicago Tribune (A&P)

The following is a listing of books that
contain information, photos, etc. about
Shirley Temple and/or Shirley Temple
dolls.

Academy Awards Illustrated. Robert
Osborne-Marvin Miller Enterprises
(P) 1965
American Movies Reference Book.
Paul Michael. Prentice Hall (P) 1969
Academy Awards, A Pictorial History.
Paul Michael. Crown Pub. 1968
American Heritage, History of the 20's
& 30's. American Heritage Pub. Co.
(P)
An Ernie Pyle Album. Lee G. Miller.
Wm. Sloane Ass'ts (P). 1946
All Talking, All Singing, All Dancing.
John Springer. Citadel Press (P)
1969
American Story. Bruce Gould. Harper
& Row. (P) 1968
All The Things We Were. Louise
Tanner. Doubleday. (P). 1968
Antique Doll Price Guide. Marlene
Leuzzi (P)
Advertised Prices of Dolls. Sylvia
Bryant. 1969
Antique Traders Price Guide. Fall 1970
America At The Movies. Margaret
Thorp. (P). 1940
America's Tastes. Longley, Silvester &
Tower. (P)
American Movies, The. Paul Michael
& Jim Parrish. Prentice Hall
Alice Faye Movie Book. Mosher. 1974
The American Musical. Tom Vallence.
C. Timling (London) 1970
Boys & Girls Film Book. Mary Field
& Maude Miller. Burke Pub. (P). 1947

Beat It, Kid, You Can't Vote. Harvey
Kurtzman. Fawcett Pub. (P). 1967
Book Of Knowledge Annual 1942
Big Broadcast 1920-1950. Frank Burton
& Bill Owen. Viking
Boys & Girls Cinema Annual. 1950
Book Of Knowledge Supplement 1939
(A&P)
Boy's Cinema Annual 1937. Fleetway
House London (P)
Boy's Cinema Annual 1936. (P)
Button Book. Ted Hoke. Dafran House
Pub. 1972
Captain January & Little Colonel. 1958.
Random House
Child Stars Dolls & Toys. Loraine
Burdick. 1968
Child Stars. N. Zicrold. Coward
McCann Inc. (P) 1965
Celebrity Register. Cleveland Amory.
(P). 1960
Confessions Of A Hollywood
Columnist. Shelah Graham
Children's Bluebird Story Book.
Whiteman #603. 1940
Cooking With Love & Paprika. Joe
Pasternak. B. Geiss Ass't. (P). 1966
Child Craft Encyclopedia 1945. Vol. 11
(P)
Complete Book Of Doll Collecting.
Helen Young
Curios & Collectables. Dafran House.
1971
Children's Hair Care. Dell Purse
Booklet #1238 (P)
Collecting Nostalgia. John Mebane
Cinema. Kenneth Leich 1974
Child Craft Encyclopedia. 1947
Compton Encyclopedia Yearbook. 1976
Collectors Guide to Depression Glass.
Hawthorn
Composition Dolls Cute & Collectable.
Rhoda Shoemaker. Vol. 1. 1974
Composition Dolls Cute & Collectable.
Rhoda Shoemaker. Vol. II. 1975
Dimples. Saalfield #1760. 1936
Directory Of U.S. Doll Trademarks.
Luella Hart. 1968
Dimples & Sawdust No. 2. Marlowe
Cooper. 1968 (P)
Don't Say Yes Until I Finish Talking.
Mel Gusson. Doubleday. (P). 1971
Doll Collector's Treasures. Laural
Dicicco (P). 1971
Dolls & Dollmakers. Mary Hillier.
G.P. Putmans.
Decline And Fall Of Hollywood. E.
Goodman. Simon & Schuster
Daily Express Film Book. Ernest
Betts. Daily Exp. Pub. (P). 1935
Debonairs. The. June Parish & D.s.
Arlington House (P). 1975
Doll's Family Album. Edna Knowles-
king. Whitman. (P). 1937
Don't Get Me Wrong, I Love
Hollywood. Sid Skolsky
Doll Collectors Treasures. Vol. II.
Laural Dicicco. 1975.
Dolls. Shirley Glubok

Doll Home Library Series. Marlowe Cooper. Vol. XXIII & XIV

A Doll For Christmas. Loraine Burdick. Quest Books. 1971

Dolls Images of Love. M. Selfridge. 1973

Dolls! Dolls! Dolls! Thelma & JoLeen Flack. 1975

Dolls, Dolls, Dolls, Shirley Glubock. Follett Pub. Co. 1975

Five Books About Me. Saalfield #1722 1936: 1730A—Shirley Temple Little Playmate; 1730B—Shirley Temple In Starring Roles; 1730C—Just A Little Girl; 1730D—Shirley Temple On The Movie Lot 1730 E.—Shirley Temple Twinkle Toes

Foods & Fashions Of 1936 (P)

First Book Of Dolls. Helen Hoke. Franklin Watts, Inc. 1954

Favorite Stories Of Famous Children. Dixie Willson. Henry Holt Co. (P) 1938

From The Crash To The Blitz. Cabell Phillips. New York Times. (P). 1969

Film Pictorial Annual of 1940. (C)

Fort Apache. French Edition (P)

Films In America. Quigley & Gertner (P)

Famous Stars Famous Food. Fannie Sniff. 1938

Foremost Films of 1938. Vreeland (P)

Filmgoers Companion

Fox Girls, The. James Parish. Arlington House. 1971

Flea Market Shopper. Dafran House

Film Review. Maurice Speed. 1948

Film Parade. Ed. by Doug. Crane & K.E. Willis. (P). 1948

Film Review 1945. Maurice Speed. (P)

Fifty Years of Movie Posters. John Kobal. Bounty Books

50 Super Stars. John Kobal. Bounty Books. 1974

Film Goers Book Of Quotes. Leslie Hallwiell. Signet Film Series. 1975

Focus On Films. No. 18. Summer 1974 (P)

Films of Gary Cooper. Homer Dickens. (P) 1971

Film Pictorial Annual 1937 (P)

Film Fun Annual 1939 (P)

FAO Schwartz Toys Through The Years. Marvin Schwartz. Doubleday. 1975

Encyclopedia Brittanica. Vol. 15. 1939

Encyclopedia Of American Dolls. Ruth Freeman. Century House

Encyclopedia Brittanica Book Of Year 1948 (P)

English In Action. 3rd Ed. Tressler (P)

Ernie Pyle Album. Lee Miller. W. Sloane. (P). 1946

Encyclopedia Of The World's Great Events. D. Shalacy, Jr. Monarch Books. 1963

Encyclopedia Yearbook. 1968. Grolier. (P)

Give Me Liberty. Nostalgia Book Club (P). 1970

Guiness Book Of World Records

Golden Home & High School Encyclopedia. Golden Press 1961. Vol. 12

Gary Cooper Story. George Caycozis Jr.

Gotta Sing, Gotta Dance. John Kobal

Great Movie Stars. The Golden Years. David Shipman (P)

Great Movies On TV. F. Friedman

Grauman's Chinese Theatre (booklet) 1943

Golden Age Of Sound Comedy. Donald McCaffrey

Glamor Girls, The. James Parrish. Arlington House. 1975

Heidi #337. Saalfield. Re-issued in 1962

Heidi #1771. Saalfield. 1937

Heidi (red binding) Saalfield 1937

Heidi (blue binding) Saalfield 1937

Heidi. Random House. 1938

How I Raised Shirley Temple. Gertrude Temple. 1935

Hollywood And The Academy Awards. Natalie Fredrich. (P). 1969

Honeymoon #103. 1947. Bartholamew House

Here Today. Louise Tanner. Thomas Crowell Co. 1959

Hollywood Hall of Fame. Johnny Roth. Richards Int. (P). 1968

Hollywood & The Great Fan Magazines. M. Levin. Arbor House. 1970

Hollywood In The Forties. Charles Higman & Joel Greenberg. (P). 1970

Here Is Your Hobby—Doll Collecting. Helen Young (P)

History Of Man's Progress. Pioneer Village

Harper's Bazaar (100 Years of the American Female) Random House. 1970

History Of Toys. Antonia Fraser. Delacorte. 1966

Hollywood Camerman. Charles Highman. Indiana U. Press

Hollywood Without Makeup. Pete Martin. Lippincott. 1948

Heart Of Hollywood. Bob Thomas

Hollywood Musical, The. Taylor & Jackson. McGraw Hill

Hollywood—London Film Parade. D. Crane & K. Willis. (P). 1948

Hartedief (Bright Eyes) Dutch

Hollywood Album. Ed. by Ivy Crane Wilson. London (P). 1948

Hollywood Album. 1949

Home University Library. Vol. 12

Hollywood Musical Picture Quiz Book. Stanley Applebaum. Dover. (P). 1974

Immortals Of The Screen. Ray Stuart. Bonanza Books. 1965

Inside Filmland. 1950. (P)

Image Makers, The. McGraw Hill (P)

I Remember Distinctly. Agnes Rogers. Harper. 1947

Ideals (Nostalgia Issue) July 1975

Jean Hersholts Album Of Hollywood Stars. 1938

Just Around The Corner. British Ed.

Kapitein Januari (Capt. January) Dutch

Littlest Rebel. Edward Peple. Dodd, Meade & Co. 1935

Littlest Rebel. Edward Peple. Random House. 1958

Littlest Rebel. Big Little Book. 1935 Saalfield. No. 1595 &1115

Little Colonel. A.L. Burt Co. 1935

Little Colonel. Big Little Book. Saalfield. 1935. No. 1095 & 1596

Little Colonel (With Capt. January) Random House. 1958

Little Miss Broadway. Saalfield 1938. #1778

The Little Princess. Saalfield 1939. #1783

Liberty Years. Allen Churchill. Prentice Hall. 1970

Longest Street. Louis Sobol. (P)

Life Goes To The Movies. Time, Inc. 1975

My Young Life (Look Mag) by Shirley Temple. 1945 Garden City Pub.

Movie Stars, The. Richard Griffith. 1970

Movies, The. Richard Griffith & Arthur Mayer. Bonanza Books (P). 1957

Movies, The. Revised 1970

Mrs. Howard Hughes. Raymond Strist

Movie Of Me, A. Flip Booklet. 1935

My Life And Times. Saalfield. #1116 &#1596. 1936

More Than Welcome. Dean Boyd. Harcourt Brace & World

Movie Moguls. Phillip French

Movie Quiz Book. M. Vance. (P)

Movieland Wax Museum Stars Hall Of Fame. 1962

Motion Picture Performers Bibliography of Magazine and Periodical Articles. 1900-1969

Movie Greats. Paul Michael & Jim Parish. Prentice Hall

Movie Review. A.E. Wilson. (P). 1948

Movies For The Millions. Gilbert Seldes. Batsford London. (P). 1937

M.G.M. Stock Co. James Parish & Ronald Bowers. Arlington House. 1973

Movies, The. A Picture Quiz Book. Stanley Applebaum & Hayward Cirher. Dover. 1972

Meet The Film Stars. 1934-5

Movie Musical

More Twentieth Century Dolls. J. Anderton. Athena. 1974

Modern Collector's Dolls. Patricia R. Smith. Collector Books. 1973

Modern Collector's Dolls. Patricia R. Smith. Collector Books. Vol. II. 1975

Modern Collector's Dolls. Patricia R. Smith. Collector Books. Vol. III. 1976

Now I Am Eight. Saalfield #1766. 1937

New Family Encyclopedia. Vol. 13. 1954

New Deal And Global War. 1964. Vol. II. Life History of U.S. Times. (P)

New Book of Knowledge. 1966. Vol. 12. (P)

New Standard Encyclopedia (P)

New Hollywood and Academy Awards. Nathalie Frederich (P)

Notes On A Cowardly Lion. Bert Lahr

Nostalgia Quiz Book. Martin Gross (P)

New York Time's Directory of the Films. (P)

Negro in Films. (P)

New International Yearbook. 1935

Of All Places. Abbe Children. Fred Stokes Co. 1937 (P)

Oscar at the Academy Awards. Robert Osborne. 1969. (P)

Our Button Book. Eliz. Daniel. Rand McNally Co. 1938

Old Dolls. Eleanor St. George. 1950

Our Wonderful World. Vol. 14. Spencer Press. Inc. 1956. (P)

1000 Makers of the Twentieth Century

Pictorial History of the Talkies. D. Blum. G.P. Putnam Sons. 1958

Pictorial History of Television. D. Blum. Chilten Co. 1959

Poor Little Rich Girl. Saalfield. #1723. 1936

Pictorial History of the Movies. Deems Taylor. 1943

Pictorial History of the Movies. Deems Taylor. 1950

Pictures of Movie Stars. Mae Tinee. Whitman. 1937 (P)

Pictorial History of the Talkies, New. D. Blum. 1970 (P)

Petite Princess Shirley Temple (French) 1939

Pictorial History of Dolls.

Playboy's "Teevee Jeebees." S. Silvester. 1963 (P)

Photoplay Treasury

Piccola Rebelle (Littest Rebal) Italy

Photographing Children. Time Life. (P)

Portrait of Dolls. Vol. II. Carol Jacobsen. 1974

Paper Dolls of Famous Faces. Jean Woodcock

Picture Story of an Unforgettable Year—1936. D. Halasy Jr. Arlington House. (P). 1963

Picture Show Annual. (P). 1939

Picture Show Annual. 1937 (P)

Picture Show Annual. 1938 (P)

Popcorn Venus. Marjorie Rosen. Avon

People. Alfred Einsenstadt. Viking. 1973

Paper Dolls & Their Artists. Mary Young

Remember When. Allen Churchill. Golden Press. 1967

Rebecca Of Sunnybrook Farm. K. Wiggin. Random House. 1958

Remember Television. Ron Lackman

Roxy Theatre Souvenir Album. 1939 (P)

Rebels. Morella & Epstein (p)

The R.K.O. Gals. James Parish. Arlington House. 1974

Rhoda Shoemaker's Price Guide For Compo. Dolls. 1973 and 1975

Story of Shirley Temple. Big Little Book. Saalfield. #1319 & 1089. 1934

Stowaway, Saalfield. #1767. 1937

Stars and Films of 1939. Daily Express Pub. (P). 1937

Shirley Temple Annual. The Daily Herald. London. 1938

Shirley Temple's Birthday Book. Dell Pub. 1935

Shirley Temple's Christmas Book. Saalfield. #1770. 1937

Shirley Temple's Story Book. Saalfield. 1935

Shirley Temple, Little Star. Saalfield. #1762. 1936

Shirley Temple Throu The Day. Saalfield. #1716. 1936

Shirley Temple At Play. Saalfield. #1712. 1935

Shirley Temple's Pastime Book. Saalfield. 1935

Shirley Temple's Book Of Fairytales. Saalfield. 1936

Shirley Temple, Her Life In Pictures. Saalfield. 1938. #1774

Susannah Of The Mounties. Saalfield. 1939

Susannah Of The Mounties. Randon House. 1958

Shirley Temple. Jerome Beatty. Saalfield. 1935

Shirley Temple. My Life And Times. Big Little Book. 1936. Saalfield #1116 &1596

Shirley Temple. Lois Eby. Monarch. 1962

Shirley Temple Dolls and Related Delights. Lorranine Burdick. 1966

Stars. Richard Schickel. Bonanza (P)

Shirley Temple and the Screaming Spectre. K. Heisenfelt. 1945 Whitman Pub.

Shirley Temple and the Spirit of Dragonwood. K. Heisenfelt. 1945. Whitman Pub.

Shirley Temple's Favorite Poems. Saalfield. #1720. 1936

Shirley Temple's Treasury. Random House. 1959

Shirley Temple's Favorite Tales of Long Ago. Random House. 1958

Shirley Temple's Stories That Never Grow Old. Random House. 1958

Shirley Temple's Fairyland. Random House. 1958

Shirley Temple's Nursery Tales. Random House. 1961

Shirley Temple's Storytime Favorites. Random House. 1962

Shirley Temple, the Real Little Girl. Saalfield. #1938. 1936

Shirley Temple's Storybook. Random House. 1958

Shirley Temple's Favorite Games. Saalfield #1732A. 1937

Shirley Temple's Bedtime Book. 1962

Shirley Temple's Pastime Box. Saalfield. 1937

Standard American Encyclopedia. Vol. 5. 1937

Story Of My Life. Shirley Temple. Fox Film Corp. 1934

Say, Didn't You Used To Be George Murphy. George Murphy. (P). 1970

Shirley Temple. Saalfield. Big Little Book. 1935

Selznick. Bob Thomas. Doubleday. 1970

Story Of Walt Disney. Diane Disney Miller. Henry Holt & Co. (P). 1956

Shirley. German edition. (Stowaway)

Story Of Dolls & How To Make New Ones. Mills & Dunn (P)

Salute To The Thirties, A.

Shirley Temple's Favorite Coloring Book. #1732D.

Sinking Of The Lollipop. Rodney Ninott. Diablo Press

Seattle 1968. U.F.D.C.

Sewing For 20th Century Dolls. Johanna Anderton

Shirley Temple's Annual. 1937. British

Stars & Films Of 1938. Daily Express Pub.

Shirley Temple Scrapbook. Lorranine Burdick. Jonathan David Pub. 1975

Selznick Players. Ronald Bowers

Shirley Temple. Robert Windeler. (British) 1976

Shirley Temple. Jeanine Basinger. Pyramid Books. 1975

Swashbucklers, The. James Parish. Arlington House Pub. 1976

Spinning Wheel's Complete Book Of Dolls. Galahad Books. 1975

Standard Modern Dolls. Collector Books. 1976

This Fabulous Century. Time-Life Books. 1969

Thousand & One Delights. Alan Barbour. (P)

Trivia. Pocket Books. 1966

Tournament Of Roses Booklet. 1-2-39 (P)

Tournament of Roses Pictorial. 1937

Those Endearing Young Charms. Marc Best. (P). 1971

Tournament Of Roses. Joe Hendrickson. (P)

Time Capsule. 1939

Una O Povera Bimba Milinaria (Italy)

Those Great Movie Ads. Arlington House. 1972

Tournament Of Roses. Hendrickson. Brooke House. 1971 (P)

Talkies, The. Photoplay. 1929-40

University Of Knowledge. 1938

Television Years. 1973. Arthur Shulman & Roger Youman. Popular Library

To Find An Image. James Murray

Those Fabulous Movie Years, The 30's. Paul Trent. Barre Pub. Co. 1975

Time Annual 1959. Year In Review (P)

Vanity Fair. 1970. Viking Press. (P)

Vanity Fair Collection Years. 1935-6. University Microfilms

Wee Willie Winkie. Saalfield #1769. 1937

World Book Annual. 1934
World Book Annual. 1935
Who's Who In America. 1961
We Were Five. James Brough. Simon
  Schuster. 1965
Will Rogers. P.J. O'Brien. 1935. (P)
Will Rogers. Big Little Book. Jerome
  Beatty. Saalfield. 1935. (P)

Why Me? William Gargan. 1969.
  Doubleday. (P)
World In Review. 1967. Associated
  Press
Warner Bros. Golden Anniversary
  Book. 1973
Year 1951 (P)

Year. Mid-Century Edition 1950.
  Year, Inc. (P)
Year 1958
Year. 1948 (P)
Year. 1954 (P)
Zanuck. Leo Guild. 1970

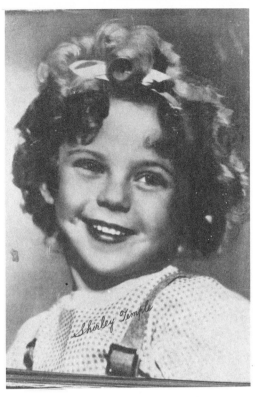

A 1930's framed give away photo.

Framed "give a way" photo.

One of the many give away photos of the 1930's.

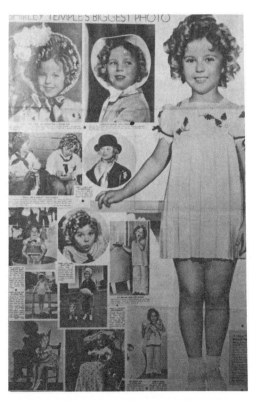

Double page of newspaper photos of Shirley in the Chicago Daily News, Jan. 18, 1936. These features were common throughout the country. This sheet measures 31½" by 21½".

117

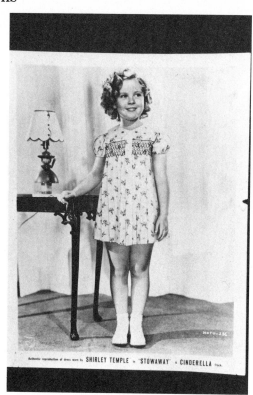

This is a photo of Shirley wearing an actual frock that was a reproduction of one worn in the movie "Stowaway" and made by Cinderella Frocks.

A framed photo of the 1930's.

Shows Shirley holding doll dressed in matching outfit and tams.

Before the actual doll's head was designed and photographed, Ideal Toy and Novelty Co. used this ad with the actual head of Shirley Temple superimposed on that of the doll.

Shirley poses with two 1950's issue of the Shirley Temple doll made by Ideal Doll Corp. The one standing is a 17" model and it has generally been rumored that a large doll was made and seems to be true, by this photo. If the doll was actually released is not known. This one appears to be about 21" to 23" tall.

This 1936 Shirley Temple doll is being shown off by Shirley herself.

This picture taken on Dec. 30, 1936 shows Shirley carrying one of her dogs, "Ching Ching." The picture was taken at the Desert Inn, Palm Springs, Calif. by International News Photo Service.

Shirley plays with her #1 pal, her dog.

119

This give away picture was to the members of the Chicago Times Shirley Temple Club. The club pin is shown at upper part of picture.

One of the numerous and varied give away photos of the famous child star.

Shirley welcomes in the year of 1935. This is a Fox Film photo by Gene Kornman.

This give away photo was Shirley's new hair style used in the movie: "Little Miss Broadway." 1938.

This movie still shows Shirley with Charles Farrell as they played in "Just Around The Corner" 1938.

Shirley in a scene from "Heidi."

Twentieth Century-Fox give away of 1938.

Give away photo by Modern Screen Magazine. 1934.

SHIRLEY TEMPLE—Fox Star

Enter VASSAR WAVER Contest
Win A Shirley Temple Doll.

SHIRLEY TEMPLE

This photo helped promote the Vassar Waver contest where nine Shirley Temple dolls were given away. The Vassar Waver was a rubber rod used to set the hair.

Best wishes for happy holidays—Shirley Temple

This photo was given with the compliments of 8 neighborhood merchants. Shows Shirley as Santa Claus.

Shows Shirley in her famous Dancing Dress beside a trunk holding a doll that wears the same designed dress. Doll clothes were designed by Mollye Goldman.

Photo of teenage Shirley. 1940's. Made during the time she was under contract with M.G.M.

This give away photo was presented by "Film Pictorial" July 31, 1937.

Upper left: No maker or number information. Upper right: Made exclusively for 20th Century-Fox by Lumitone, U.S.A. Dated 1937. Lower left: Same marked card but in different colors. Lower right: No maker or number information.

Upper left: Robert Kashower càrd #713 and shows the bungalow dressing room of Shirley Temple. Upper right: Western Publishers Card #810. Shows Shirley's first home. Lower left: Rober Kashower card #788. Shows second home in Brentwood Heights, Calif. Lower right: Gardner-Thompson Co. card #127. Shows bungalow dressing room.

Upper left: Western Publishers & Novelty Co. #810 Home of Shirley Temple. Upper right: Same postcard with different photo insert. Lower left: Same post card with different photo insert. Lower right: Tichnor Art Co. #T374.

Upper: Mitock & Sons "Plastichrome." Shows Grauman's Chinese Theatre. Lower: Same.

Upper left: Carte Postale by IPA/CT #10776. Upper right: no marks. Lower left: U.S.A. by EKC. No numbers. Lower right: From the Selznick Studio, Culver City, Calif.

Upper left: Angeleno Photo Service, L.A., Calif. No series number. Upper right: Angeleno Photo Service, L.A., Calif. No series number. Lower left: England. No series number. Lower right: No maker or number information.

Upper left: Just marked C.C.M. 27. Upper right: German marked: HEMO. No number. Lower left: From the Vanguard Studio, Culver City, Calif. #ST426. Lower right: From Vanguard Studio, Culver City, Calif. No number.

Upper left: From the Selznick Studio, Culver City, Calif. Upper right: Movie Candid Color Card, Beverly Hills, Calif. No series number. Lower left: Marked copyright No. 3219. Lower right: No. W150 of "Picturegoer" series. England.

Upper left: Shirley Temple Agar. U.S.A. Upper right: England No. W560 of the "Picturegoer" Series. Lower left: England. No series number. Lower right: U.S.A. From Shirley Temple's former office in Los Angeles.

Upper left: U.S.A. No series number. Upper right: German, Series #3070. Lower left: Vanguard Studio, Culver City, Calif. No series number. Lower right: No information.

#208 Shirley Temple "Poster Card" made by Trilby Posters, Venice, Calif. Measures 8 x 5.

Upper left: England. "Picturegoer" Series No. 841. Upper right: From 20th Century-Fox Studios. From 20th Century-Fox during World Premiere at Carthay Circle Theatre in Los Angeles of "Wee Willie Winkie" Lower right: England Colorgraph Series No. C289.

This 8 x 5½" post card was made in 1971 by Portal Publications, Ltd. Sausalito, Calif. 94965.

125

Upper left: Holland S3 Upper right: England "Picturegoer" Series No. 1019. Lower left: England "Picturegoer" Series No. 841b. Lower right: England "Picturegoer" Series No. 841c.

Upper left: England "Picturegoer" Series No. 997. Upper right: England Picturegoer Series No. 988. Lower left: England "Picturegoer" Series No. 942. Lower right: England "Picturegoer" Series No. 942a.

Upper left: England "Picturegoer" Series No. 1007. Upper right: England "Picturegoer" Series No. 1020. Lower left: England "Picturegoer" Series No. 1020a. Lower right: England "Picturegoer" Series No. 1019a.

Upper left: England #64.B. Upper right: England #64.D. Lower left: England #64. Lower right: England #64.F.

Upper left: England Photogravure Portrait. No series number. Upper right: No maker or number information. Lower left: England #64-G. Lower right: England #64-1.

Upper left: England #64-0. Upper right: England #64-K. Lower left: England #64-H Lower right: England #7195.

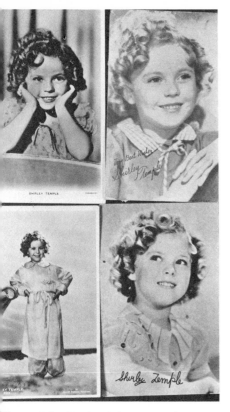

Upper left: England Colourgraph Series No. C224. Upper right: No marks. Lower left: Enerett Brodrene Halvorsen #16. Lower right: Photogravure England. No number.

Upper left: England. Colourgraph Series No. C409. Upper right: U.S.A. Photo credit to J. Gray of L.A. Lower left: No marks. Lower right: Holland. No series number.

Upper left: England No. FS107. Upper right: England No. FS106. Lower left: England No. FS103. Lower right: England No. FS41.

Upper left: England No numbers. Upper right: England. No. FS133. Lower left: England No. FS134. Lower right: England. No numbers.

Upper left: England. Series No. B.1. Upper right: U.S.A. No series number. Lower left: This postcard is from Shirley Temple to her fans thanking them for writing. Lower right: No information.

Upper left: Ad postcard for Playhouse, Wakefield. 1936. Upper right: England Film Partners Series No. PC 179. Lower left: England No. FS8. Lower right: England "Valentine" #7193.

127

Upper left: England No. FS31. Upper right: England No. 64-L. Lower left: England No. 64-J. Lower right: England No. FS38.

Upper left: England No. FS40. Upper right: England No. FS36. Lower left: England No. FS35. Lower right: England No. FS33.

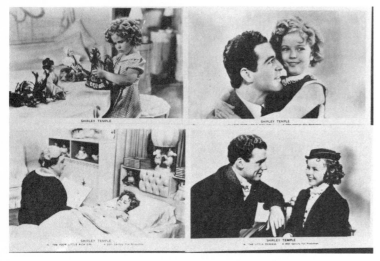

Upper left: England No. FS39. Upper right: England No. FS37. Lower left: England No. FS32. Lower right: England No. FS185.

Upper left: Stars Hall of Fame, Orlando, Fla. #B5676. Upper right: Movieland Wax Museum, Buena Park, Calif. #B1649. Lower: Also Movieland Wax Museum, Buena Park Calif. #76614-B.

Upper left: England. Colourgraph Series No. C291. Upper right: England No. FS182. Lower left: England No. FS54. Lower right: England No. FS115.

Upper left: England No. FS142. Upper right: England No. FS145. Lower left: England No. FS143. Lower right: England No. FS144.

Upper left: England No. FS138. Upper right: England No. FS139. Lower left: England No. FS140. Lower right: England No. FS141.

Upper left: England No. FS146. Upper right: England No. FS147. Lower left: England No. FS148. Lower right: England No. FS30.

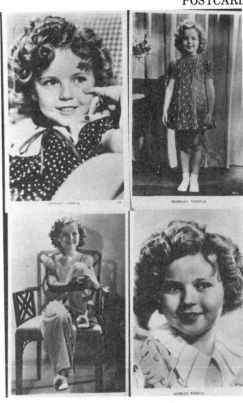

Upper left: England Picturegoer Series No. 997. Upper right: England Art Photo #41L. Lower left: England Art Photo #41S Lower right: England Art Photo #41N.

Upper left: England. No numbers. Upper right: England No. FS136. Lower left: England No. FS152. Lower right: England. No numbers.

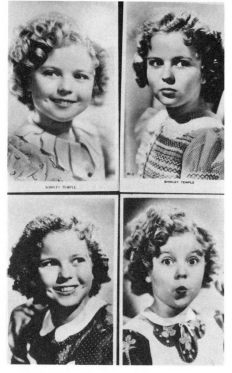

Upper left: England Art Photo #41-B.
Upper right: England Art Photo #41-11.
Lower left: England Art Photo #41-9.
Lower right: England Art Photo #41-D.

Upper left: England Art Photo #41-5.
Upper right: England Art Photo #41-C.
Lower left: England Art Photo #41-2.
Lower right: England Art Photo #41-A.

Upper left: England Art Photo #41-1.
Upper right: England Art Photo #41-H.
Lower left: England Art Photo #41-1.
Lower right: England Art Photo #41-P.

Upper left: England No. FS151. Upper right: England No. FS150. Lower left: England No. FS135. Lower right: England No. FS137.

Upper left: England No. FS149. Upper right: Ediciones Bistagne: Series 1, #6. Lower left: Card by LaVaughn Johnston, Downey, Calif. Currently available. Lower right: Card printed for "A Doll's World" (exclusively). Currently available.

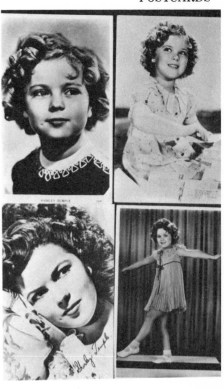

Upper left: England "Milton" series #64.E. Upper right: England #93. Lower left: England #64.a. Lower right: No marks.

Upper left: England: Valentines. #7187. Upper right: England #7190C. Lower left: England "Valentines" #7190E. Lower right: England Picturegoer Series No. 841a.

Upper left: England #7241. Upper right: Tarjeta Postal. No series number. Lower left: No maker or number information. Lower right: England "Valentine" #7195.

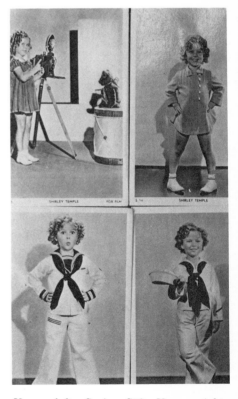

Upper left: Holland S8. Upper right: Holland S9. Lower left: Holland S1. Lower right: Holland S2.

Upper left: Holland Series S12. Upper right: Holland Series S7. Lower left: By Ross Verlag. No series number. Lower right: Ross Verlag with #A1809/3.

Upper left: Series S13. Upper right: Series S14. Lower left: Series S15. Lower right: Series S11. All are from Holland set.

131

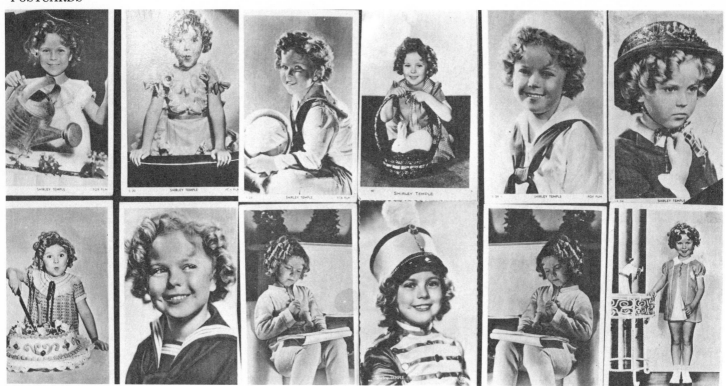

Upper left: S22. Upper right: S20. Lower left: S21. Lower right: S16. All from Holland.

Upper left: Holland #S28. Upper right: Carte Postale #41. Lower left: Holland #S31. Lower right: Chantal Collection, Paris. #41a.

Upper left: #S39. Upper right: #S35. Lower left: #S32. Lower right: #S30. All from Holland.

Upper left: Holland #S4. Upper right: No maker nor number information. Lower left: Holland #S5. Lower right: England. Picturegoer Series No. 1394.

Upper left: S48. Upper right: S49. Lower left: S44. Lower right: S46. All from Holland.

Upper left: Holland S42. Upper right: Holland S38. Lower left: England "Picturegoer" Series No. 1007a. Lower right: England Picturegoer Series No. 997a.

Upper left: S52. Upper right: S53. Lower left: S54. Lower right: S55. All from Holland.

All four are Italian Postcards. No series numbers.

Upper left: Holland #S45. Upper right: Stamped Nederland Helpt Indie. Lower left: England. No. FS104. Lower right: England No. FS105.

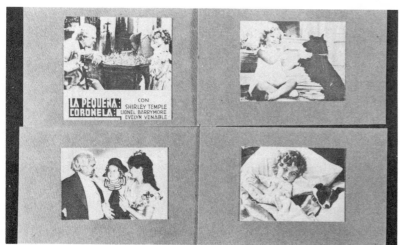

All four are "Cartolina Postales" from Italy.

Upper left: Ross Vertag #A1237/2. Upper right: Ross Vertag #9132/1. Lower left: Ross Vertag #9425/5. Lower right: Ross Vertag #A1258/1.

Upper left: Ross Vertag #9730/1. Upper right: Ross Vertag #1639/1. Lower left: Ross Vertag #1639/3. Lower right: Ross Vertag #9425/5.

Upper left: Ross Vertag. Other side h stamp of the 1936 Olympic Games Berlin. Upper right: Ross Vertag #A148 1. Lower left: Ross Vertag #9425/6. Low right: Holland. No series number.

Upper left: Marked: Forte. No numbers. Upper right: No marks. Lower left: Ross Vertag #2325/3. Lower right: Holland #S47.

Upper left: German Series #10768. Upper right: French Series #107. Lower left: France Series #657. Lower right: Holland. No series number on card.

Upper left: Carte Postale by IPA/ #10749. Upper right: Same, #10759. Lo left: German series #17. Lower ri German, series #18.

Upper left: Ediciones Series 1 #4. Upper right: Ediciones Series 1 #5. Lower left: Spain. Josep Colomer. #1. Lower right: Ediciones Series 1 #1.

Upper left: Ediciones Series 1 #3. Upper right: Ediciones Series 1 #1. Lower left: Ediciones Series 1 #2. Lower right: Ediciones Series 1 #2.

Upper left: Germany. Metropole. No series number. Upper right: Tichnor Art Co. #T267. Lower left: Western Publishers & Novelty Co. Shows Shirley's block at the Grauman's Chinese Theatre. Lower right: U.S.A. No maker or number information.

Upper left: Series A No. 1, Spain. Upper right: Series A No. 3 Spain. Lower left and right: No maker or series information.

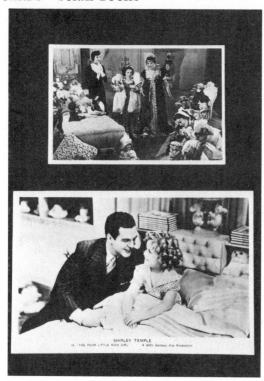

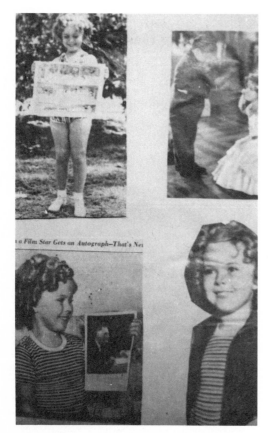

Right: Spanish postcard #4256 by Archvio Bermego. Right one is unmarked.

Top: This is a tradecard for Max Cigarettes. It is a scene from "Bluebird." Lower: England No. FS30.

ALL ITEMS FROM MEISINGER COLLECTION UNLESS NOTED

A scrapbook page that shows Shirley reading the funnies and holding an autographed photo of President Roosevelt.

Here Shirley is shown visiting with Sonja Henie.

A typical Scrapbook page on Shirley and shows her "growth chart," her dog and strolling with buggy and doll.

Another typical page from a scrapbook.

Scrapbook by Western Printing Co. 1962.

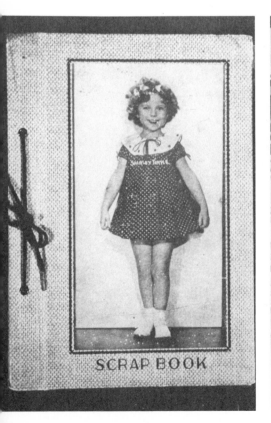

A scrapbook of the 1930's.

Pages from a typical Shirley Temple Scrapbook.

These are pages from Shirley Temple scrapbooks. Lower right courtesy Sandy Crump.

These are the fronts of the tags on Nanette fashions of the 1930's.

Top cards were given with Trimfit socks. Lower left is the front and back of a tag with Shirley Temple hats. Right tag came with Shirley Temple coats.

These are the backs of some of the fashion tags by Nanette. 1930's.

Tags from composition dolls: Woven cotton: Shirley Temple/Doll dress/Reg. U.S. Pat. Off./Ideal Nov. & Toy Co. along with NRA, eagle and code, plus vertical: Made in U.S.A. The other tag is cotton backed nylon: Genuine Shirley Temple/doll/registered U.S. Pat. Off./Ideal Nov. & Toy Co. along with the vertical: Made in U.S.A.

This original doll has a slightly different pin and dress tag. The tag is nylon that is stamped: Genuine Shirley Temple (signature)/Doll dress/trademark registered/Ideal Nov. & Toy Co. With NRA code. Pin: The World's Darling-Genuine Shirley Temple Doll. A different pose than most original pins.

The 1973 Shirley dresses carry the tag: Shirley Temple TM/1973 Ideal Toy Corp./ Hollis NY 11423/dress made in Hong Kong. Printed.

This is a tag from a dress of the 1957 issue of Shirley Temple in vinyl: Shirley Temple/made by Ideal (in oval) Toy Corp. Tag is printed on nylon.

Upper: No. 8 in collection of 21 cards, Spain. Lower: No. 13 in collection of 21 cards, Spain.

Series B Number 7 in a Spanish set of collectors' cards.

All the cards shown have no information or numbers printed on them.

Upper left: Gallaher Ltd. England "Curly Top" Series of 48. #33. Upper middle: Gallaher Ltd. England "Now and Forever" Series of 48 #39. Upper right: Gallaher Ltd. England. "Our Little Girl" Series of 48 #5. Lower left: Ross Vertag. No series numbers. Lower middle: Belgian Chewing Gum Ltd. Antwerp. Lower right: only has #X72 on it.

Top: No. 29 in series of 50 issued by Godfrey Phillips Ltd. England. Middle is No. 26 in series of 50 issued by Stephen Mitchell & Sons. No. 163 of the Holland series. Lower: No. 22 in series of 50 by Carreras Ltd. England. Middle: W.T. Grant card issued by weight machine. Next is No. 25 in series of 48 by Godfrey Phillips Cig. Co. England.

141

Foreign trade cards. Top: Series A #93, W.B. #D11, W.B. C29. Lower: W.B. #C8 #26, #52. All are from Holland and are cigarette cards.

Top: Candy card, photo by Ross Vertag. Second photo is also by Vertag and comes from Holland. Lower: No. 86 in a series of 96. Issued by Carreras Limited, England. Next is No. 27 in series of 50 issued by Oden Tobacco Co. Last is No. 44 in series of 96 issued by Carreras, Ltd. England. All are cigarette manufacturers.

These cards are from Holland. Top: No. 148 and 132. Lower: No. 145 and 139.

Top three are No. 9, 26 and 83 in a series from Holland. Lower left: Cigarette card #120, series unknown. Center is No. 111 of Holland set and last is #3, series unknown.

Shows four trade cards from cigarettes. Holland.

Upper left: Printed in Holland. #11⋅ Upper right: Holland #131. Lower lef Holland #114. Lower right: Holland #11

The largest one is from Holland. Top smaller one is also from Holland and un-marked. Lower one is No. 45 in series of 50 by Ardath Tobacco Co. Ltd. England.

Top: No. 247 issued by Lloyd Cigarettes, Holland. Middle is No. 498 of the Lloyd set. Right is No. 500 by Caid Cigarettes, Holland. Lower left: No. 245 of Lloyd set and right is No. 244 of Lloyd set. Middle is No. 6 in unknown series.

ALL ITEMS FROM MEISINGER COLLECTION UNLESS NOTED

Top: Shelby Gum Co. Card No. 31. No. 2 or Mirim, Holland series. Lower: All three cards from Holland. Union candy.

All cards from Holland. Top: No. 39 and 24. Lower: No. 170 and 8.

SHIRLEY TEMPLE DOLLS AND COLLECTABLES PRICE GUIDE

The following prices are based on the knowledge of the Shirley Temple market by Mrs. Marge Meisinger and also on recent items sold through doll shows and antique shows.

PAGE 9 - Dolls. All composition and marked: 13" -$75.00, 20" -$85.00, Boxes only - $5.00 each, 11" -$140.00, 22" -$85.00

PAGE 10 - Dolls. All composition and marked: 15" -$85.00, 13" -$75.00, 18" - $85.00, 27" - $200.00

PAGE 11 - 18" - $85.00, Trunk only - $35.00, Trunk & 13" -$115.00, 20" - $85.00, 13" - $75.00 16" - $85.00, 16" -$85.00

PAGE 12 - 18" - $85.00, 18" Little Colonel - $125.00, 16" Little Colonel/box - $125.00, 13" - $75.00, 18" -$85.00, 18" -$85.00

PAGE 13 - 25" - $185.00, 11"/box - $140.00, 13" -$95.00, (Curly Top), 13" - $95.00 (Curley Top), 18" -$85.00, 27" -$200.00

PAGE 14 - 17" - $95.00 (Baby Take a Bow), 13" -$75.00, 18" -$85.00, 18" - $85.00, 13" - $75.00, 13" -$95.00 (Capt. January)

PAGE 15 - 17"/trunk - $150.00, 16" Baby - $125.00, 13"/trunk -$115.00, 27" - $200.00, 11" - $160.00 (Cowgirl)

PAGE 16 - 13" - $75.00, 16" - $85.00, 11" - $140.00, 18" -$85.00, 22" - $95.00

PAGE 17 - 18" Hawaiian - $140.00, 16" - $85.00, 22" -Cloth body -$300.00

PAGE 18 - Mechanical Shirley 27" - $1,500.00, Shirley at organ -$1,200.00

PAGE 19 - 11" Snow White - $75.00, 18" Snow White -$85.00, 20" Littlest Rebel - $120.00, Vinyl 12" -$35.00 with box, 15" vinyl -$35.00, 15" vinyl - $35.00

PAGE 20 - 35" vinyl - $365.00

PAGE 21 - 15" vinyl - $35.00, 15" vinyl - $35.00, 12" vinyl/box -$25.00, 15" vinyl - $35.00, 12" vinyl -$25.00 each, 12" vinyl Capt. January - $35.00

PAGE 22 - 12" vinyl - $25.00 each, 15" vinyl - $35.00 each, 12" vinyl - $25.00 each, 12" vinyl - $25.00 each, 12" vinyl -$25.00 each, 15" vinyl - $35.00

PAGE 23 - 35" vinyl - $365.00

PAGE 24 - 16" vinyl - $20.00 each, 15" vinyl - 1972 -$25.00, 16" store display - $20.00, 18" - 1934 - $85.00, 17" - 1934 -$85.00, 1973 16" vinyl - $20.00

PAGE 25 - 5" Soap Shirley - 2 figures - $30.00, Soap from old candy mold - $10.00, 5" Soap 'on Parade' -$20.00, 1936 Charm bracelet - $50.00 up, Cameo type -1930's $10.00, 7" recent ceramic figure -$8.00

PAGE 26 - 1930's doll pins - $9.00 to $25.00

PAGE 27 - 1930's charms - $25.00, 1930's enameled pin -$30.00, Recent watches - $15.00 up, Shrink Art pin -$4.00, 1961 jewelry on card -$20.00

PAGE 28 - Ceres medals: no known prices. Newer pins & lockets -$3.00 to $6.00, Celluloid mirror and pins -$15.00 up, Undated pin -$6.00, Mirrors with celluloid frames -$15.00 up

PAGE 29 - Nanette dress of 1930's - $15.00 up, Nanette dress of 1960's - $5.00 up Cinderella dress of 1960's -$5.00 up

PAGE 30 - Cinderella dress of 1960 - $5.00 up, Trimfit socks 1930's -$15.00, handkerchiefs - $10.00 each, gloves of 1930's -$20.00 up, purses 1930's - $20.00 up, hairbow 1930's - $15.00, Tiara 1960's -$10.00

PAGE 31 - Blue bowl - $15.00, Blue mug - $20.00, The SHORTER pitcher is rare one - $30.00, Taller pitcher -$15.00, Pink plastic tea set -$30.00

PAGE 32 - Sweet Peas - $4.00, TV Theatre - $20.00, Playing Cards - $15.00 deck

PAGE 33 - Sewing Card - $20.00, Stationary boxes -$15.00 each, Composition books and tablets - $10.00 each, Fountain pens - $20.00 each, Work with Yarn -$15.00, Treasure Board - $10.00

PAGE 35 - Misc. magazines - $5.00 each, Movie Magazines - $6.00 each, TV Guides - $4.00 each

PAGE 36 - Magazines - $5.00 up, Small display poster -$10.00, Tall poster (6 feet tall) - $100.00, Lobby photo or portfolio drawings -$10.00, Newspaper magazine sections - $5.00 up, Mid Week Pictorial (British) - $7.50

PAGE 37 - Posters (ads) - $15.00 up, Lobby Stills & Cards - $10.00 up, Wheaties set - $30.00 for set of 12

PAGE 38 - Paperdoll set #2112 - $25.00 up, Framed & dressed paperdoll - $10.00, Saalfield statuette 8" - $20.00 up, 9½" -$20.00 up, Boxed Playhouse Set - $20.00 up

PAGE 39 - 16" paperdoll - $25.00 up, #1761 - $25.00 up

PAGE 40 · #303 - $25.00 up, Spanish set - $8.00, #2425 -$15.00, Paperdoll/movie wardrobe - $25.00 up, Giveaway figurette - $10.00, #300 paperdoll - $30.00

PAGE 41 · #1348 - #4435 - #1348 - $10.00 up, #1715 -$25.00 up

PAGE 42 · Jack & Jill reprint - $5.00, $1725. - #1789 -$10.00 up, #2425 - $20.00 up, #2112 - $25.00 up, Modern paperdolls - $4.00 each set

PAGE 43 · #1768 - $10.00 up, #1772 - $10.00 up, #1711 -$10.00 up, Saalfield 1935 - $10.00, #1554 - $5.00 up, #1654 - $5.00 up, Birthday Book - $25.00 up, #1717 -$10.00 up, #1784 - $10.00 up

PAGE 44 · #4884 - 5653 - 4624 - $5.00 each

PAGE 45 · Sheet Music - $7.00 up, Hollywood Dance Folio - $8.00, Song Albums - $15.00 up. French - $20.00 up

PAGE 46 · Shirley Temple at Play - $15.00, "Shirley Temple" by Jerome Beatty - $10.00 up, Phonograph records #3006 & #FEP 100 -$10.00 up, Bambi records - $15.00, Records made in England - $5.00 up

PAGE 47 · Hard cover books - $10.00 up, Poems - $7.00, Big Little Books - $8.00 up, Soft covers #1771 - #1762 -#1760 - $12.00 up, #1778 - #1785 - #1783 & #1789 -$12.00 up

PAGE 48 · Books - My Young Life - $15.00, Hard covers -$6.00, Paperbacks - $4.00, Treasury books - $8.00 each, Random House -$5.00 each

PAGE 49 · Shirley Temple Scrap Books - $8.00 up depending on condition and amount of Shirley material in them. Safety Films - $15.00, Movie Komics - $15.00, Keystone movies - $15.00

PAGE 50 · Ken Films - $5.00, Tournament of Roses booklets - $6.00 each, Cotton material and wrapping paper - $4.00 each, Tablet - $5.00 R.C. Fan - $10.00, Calendar - $5.00

PAGE 51 · Cigar Band - $15.00, Sewing Machine - $12.00, String holder - $12.00, British Movie stamps - $4.00 each, Pencil box -$20.00, Paper mask - $15.00

PAGE 52 · Giveaway booklet - $5.00, Flip booklet - $8.00, Book of Fairy Tales - $15.00

PAGE 53 · #1712 - #1723 - #945 & #1716 - $8.00, Set #1730 - $35.00, Star & Films of 1937 - $20.00. #1775 - #337 -#1771 & #1734 - $8.00 each

PAGE 54 · Hard covers - $20.00 up, Little Princess -$10.00, German program - $8.00, Book by Jeanine Basinger - still available

PAGE 55 · Book by Lorraine Burdick - still available, Current books available, Quest books all available

PAGE 56 · 32'' high buggy - $45.00 up, 34'' buggy - $45.00 up, Wicker buggy - $60.00 up

PAGE 57 · McCall pattern - $6.00 up, Hairbow card -$6.00, Slippers box - $10.00

PAGE 58 · Trimfit socks - $5.00, Nanette dress - $5.00

PAGE 60 · 27'' composition - $200.00 if original, 18'' Mint Bluebird -$150.00, 13'' - $75.00, 13'' in trunk - $115.00

PAGE 61 · 19'' vinyl - $65.00, 17'' vinyl - $45.00, 15'' vinyl -$35.00

PAGE 62 · 15'' vinyl - $35.00, 17'' vinyl - $45.00, 36'' vinyl -$365.00

PAGE 63 · 7½'' composition - $40.00, 9'' composition -$60.00 up, 6½'' bisque - $25.00, 6½ bisque - $25.00

PAGE 64 · 4'' bisque - $55.00, recent 16'' bisque - $45.00, 13'' recent bisque - $35.00 - 23'' $75.00

PAGE 65 · 13'' - $45.00, 18'' Miss Charming - $65.00, Pin -$4.00, 19'' Nancy - $65.00

PAGE 66 · 20'' - $45.00, 17'' - $45.00, 18'' - $45.00, 19'' -$45.00

PAGE 67 · 16'' - $45.00, 18'' - $45.00, 17'' vinyl -$20.00, Outfits -$5.00 each

PAGE 68 · 18'' Cinderella - $85.00, 14½'' Bright Star -$65.00, 19'' Little Miss Movie Star - $65.00

PAGE 69 · Full page ad - $7.00, English ad - $3.00, 1956 ad -$2.00

PAGE 70 · Boxed outfits: 1930's - $15.00 up, 1950's -$5.00 up

PAGE 71 · 1930's shoes - $5.00 pair

PAGE 72 · 1950's shoes $5.00, 1930's shoe bag/shoes/socks -$20.00, Wooden rack - $15.00, 1930's cardboard hangers - $5.00

PAGE 73 · Premier shoes - $3.00, Patterns $6.00 up for 1930's, 1950's - $3.00 up

PAGE 74 · Boxed outfits - $5.00 up, Premier outfits -$3.00 up

PAGE 75 · 1960 outfits - $3.00 up, Coats - $3.00 up, Pot holder -$4.00, Embroidery set - $8.00

PAGE 76 · Embroidery set #301 - $8.00, #311 - $8.00, 1967 Political pins - $10.00 each